The YOU In Business

How to Build A Strong
Business from the Inside Out

Timothy A. Dimoff

Timothy A. Dimoff
Publisher

THE YOU IN BUSINESS

SECOND PRINTING 2000

FIRST EDITION
Copyright © 1997 by
Timothy A. Dimoff

Library of Congress Catalog Card Number: 96-92916

ISBN 0-7880-0922-2   PRINTED IN U.S.A.

Acknowledgments

This book is dedicated to my wife, Michelle, and to our children, Jenny, Darrin, and Danielle, who have supported me throughout my business career and have been an integral support in my success in the corporate environment. Without them my successful business career and this book would never have become reality.

Additionally, I would like to acknowledge my parents, Mary and George Dimoff, and my in-laws, Delores and Ralph Snyder, for their strong support and guidance.

"Success starts with a dream, and only becomes reality when followed with relentless persistence."

T.A. Dimoff

Table Of Contents

The YOU In Business

If you build your business correctly, they will come! The key to your business is definitely **YOU**! **Your** attitude, **Your** leadership, **Your** hard work, **Your** decisions, **Your** work habits, **Your** work ethics, **Your** desire for success, **Your** ability to overcome obstacles, **Your** organizational abilities, **Your** ability to make decisions and, most of all, **Your** desire to accept nothing but success!

I approached an old man one day before I decided to start my business. He said that the world was constantly changing, and that technology and the business environment were changing just as fast. He stressed one factor that will always make a difference in the success of any business. He explained that clients like to do business with people they personally know, people they personally like and people they have met. He stressed the importance of being able to put a face with a name. He said that there is only one method to ensure that this important facet of business takes place.

The old man was right. The simple recipe to business success is:

MEET PEOPLE
MEET PEOPLE
MEET PEOPLE

I built my business, my company's marketing strategy, my company's growth, my company's success and my company's strong reputation around this old man's philosophy. In fact, in every office in my building you will see a sign on the wall (Meet People-Meet People-Meet People) that describes the SACS Consulting business philosophy. It is the key to my business and personal success.

In 1991, after 14 years of service, I was forced to retire from the Akron, Ohio police department. My career-ending injuries at age 34 caused me to re-examine my entire future and the future of my family. I was awarded a small disability payment, but not nearly enough to support a wife, three children, monthly bills and a secure retirement.

I decided to build a diversified consulting business from the ground up. I had no formal business education or corporate experience. I did have an attitude and desire to succeed with no thought of not achieving that goal! Many of the things I did building my business were from trial and error experience, guidance from others and studying people who were successful in the business community. I set goals for myself that others thought I had no chance of achieving. I never forgot what the old man had said; I planted his message in my mind. I have worked towards this goal every day that I have been in business. I decided that every day possible, I would meet people, meet people, meet people!

I knew that many factors would determine my level of success. I then decided to have one main goal which would inspire me beyond anyone's wildest dreams — even mine. The single large goal I established for myself was to be a million dollar company within five years. My first year (1991), I grossed under $50,000. By 1995, I reached my million dollar goal. SACS Consulting had reached another level beyond my wildest dreams: an 8,000 square foot corporate facility with 150 full-time and part-time employees.

Is **Bigger Always Better**? Once I achieved my million dollar goal I had to examine this concept. The need for a much larger cash flow, payroll concerns, my time constraints, and several other concerns sent me back to the drawing and review boards concerning my business. I needed to review all aspects and all divisions of my business. This is not unusual, but sound business practice if you want to survive in the ever-changing business community.

The changes I needed to make at the end of my five year review were major. I would never have dreamed a few years earlier that I would be making these changes in order to grow and survive in the business world.

I discovered that I needed to sell a profitable division of SACS becaue of the strain it placed on my cash flow. Additionally, when I accounted for all the time, personnel issues, overhead, etc. that were indirectly related to this division, I discovered that it was not a profitable division. It absorbed too much of my time and was holding back the growth of my other divisions.

I also realized that my current building of 8,000 square feet was too large. I was renting part of it out and playing landlord and Mr. Maintenance. This also took away from my focus and the company focus. Finally, I had to make a few needed personnel changes and get the right team working together.

I did not hesitate to make the changes. I sold my 8,000 square foot building and moved into a 2,000 square foot facility capable of achieving the same results. I sold my Uniform Security Division and made the needed personnel changes. I structured my new personnel's income with a combination of base pay, percentages and bonuses. I employed only personnel who liked, wanted and were comfortable with this type of income structure. The positive results of these changes were very dramatic and unleashed the future growth of my company!

I had my share of both solid employees and problem employees over the building years of my business. Several employees were very dedicated and hard working, but one employee in particular had a major impact on the new direction and growth of my company. He was able to make a major impact because of his extra strong sense of the "nuts and bolts" of business. He had previously had a business of his own and understood many of the business intricacies and decisions I was contemplating. He provided me with both potential objective financial numbers and potential business results for each specific aspect of the business I was reviewing. This employee's strength in these two areas made a significant impact on my business, my life and the future of my company. He has tremendous expertise and knowledge in these specific areas of building a viable business and sustaining future growth. His name is Dave Nicholson and, for these reasons, he is the only person listed as an official contributor to this business book. We hope it will make a difference for any business person who reads it, learns from it and follows the...

Business Road Map To Success

Lesson #1: Meet People - Meet People - Meet People

I Never Have Time To Meet People

I grew up with another kid, Gary, who was a few years younger than me. Gary had always told me he had a great deal of admiration for me and liked my positive attitude. I was very flattered by his kind words and respect for me. I always took the opportunity to guide him in the right direction when he was younger. Quite frankly, I took a strong liking to Gary. I saw much potential in him.

I had not seen Gary for over 15 years. One day I received a phone call and, to my delight, it was a voice from the past — Gary. I was excited to hear from him and we decided to meet for lunch. I sensed from our conversation that he had some specific need or concern in mind. So, the lunch date was set and we ended the phone conversation with enthusiasm at the prospect of seeing each other once again.

I had been featured in a large business article in the *Beacon Journal* newspaper the week that Gary originally contacted me by phone. In the article I was described as the "guru of networking." The article explained all the personal contacts I had made, my tracking and networking methods, the success I had achieved, how my company had grown very rapidly, etc. Gary's wife had read the article, showed it to him and suggested he contact me for some guidance.

When we met for lunch, Gary explained that he was bored with his job and wanted to know how he could rekindle the fire. Second, he needed to know what he could do to meet more potentially interested customers. He felt that cold calling was not a highly successful method and it was starting to wear on him.

Gary explained to me that he made a certain number of cold calls per week with the usual low percentage of success. I don't think the results bothered him much since most business people involved in cold calling fully realize and accept the very low return on this activity.

11

The main problem for Gary was that he was dreading the cold call. It had become a totally negative experience. I proceeded to explain that in his business he still needed to make cold calls, but he also needed to use other methods of seeking potential new clients. I informed him that he needed to get out and meet people in person! I further explained that meeting people in person breaks up the monotonous routine of cold calling. It gives you an opportunity to sell yourself and *then* your business services. Remember: People desire to do business with people they *know, like* and *have met*. The people you meet in person may not need your services, but people *they* know may need your services. Everyone you meet has family, neighbors, business contacts, etc. who are all potential clients for you! It is not necessarily who you know or meet that is important, but it is who *they* know that can be crucial to your current and future growth!

To illustrate this point I will tell you one of several true incidents that I experienced concerning this theory. When I first started my business I had the opportunity to help a young man in his early twenties who was experiencing some personal problems which were affecting his personal and business future. The time I took to help him had a positive impact in his life. He made it well known to his family that I had lent my hand to help him. He told me that someday he would repay me for my time, effort, and kindness. I explained that he neither owed me nor did I expect repayment except for him to lead a positive life.

Several years later I received a call from this young man. He stated that his uncle wanted to meet with me concerning a business matter. A meeting was set up for the three of us to meet at a restaurant in a very prestigious hotel. Unknown to me, the uncle was the multi-millionaire owner of a national hotel chain. The first thing the uncle said was that he wanted to personally thank me for all my time and effort in helping his nephew five years earlier. He then discussed his needs and asked for me to handle the problem and send him the bill. It was that short and simple. To this day I still provide personal service to this national hotel chain.

I could write volumes about incidents in which I have been contacted and the conversation began with, "You don't know me" or "You never met me, but so-and-so suggested that I contact you..."

Gary's situation is not unusual in today's fast-paced business environment. Gary explained he didn't have time to meet people as I was suggesting. He said that his schedule was jammed with business meetings, planning sessions, strategy sessions, marketing sessions, etc.

I then suggested to Gary that he needed to join a few business organizations that have monthly luncheons and/or breakfast meetings. He said that he had no time for these meetings. How could he fit them into his schedule? He opened his time planner to show me his busy schedule. I was glad to see that he was busy, but why couldn't Gary and numerous other business people make better use of their time? I explained to Gary that he was NOT scheduling backwards! He was shocked at what I told him. He didn't understand.

I had him turn to the current month and asked him to schedule me for another appointment on the 10th at noon. He looked and said he already had an appointment. I said, "Schedule me for the 15th at 2:00 P.M." Gary once again said he couldn't because he already had an appointment.

I then told Gary to turn to three months from now and see if the same dates and times were available. He said both were open. I explained to Gary that he was now scheduling backwards.

I asked Gary if most meetings with other business people have to take place exactly on the date and time you schedule them. He said few of the appointments required the exact date and time at which he'd scheduled them. I then asked if the professional business organizations have specific dates and times for their meetings. He said they did.

I explained to Gary that the simple answer is to schedule, a year in advance, the regular dates/times and then schedule all other appointments, as each are requested, around those specific meeting dates/times. I schedule all regular professional business groups meetings *first* on my new calendar and daytimer (commitment book). Now when people call to schedule a meeting I can easily work around my regular meetings. Once in a while I will have a conflict and have to skip a business meeting. But I seldom miss the regular meetings...I get to *meet people* on a regular basis.

Gary decided that he would schedule his monthly appointments as he went along and then attend the regular meetings only if nothing else got scheduled at those dates/times. When I explained this system to Gary he was amazed at how easy it was and even more impressed that he still could maintain his regular schedule, but maximize his ability to meet people at several more monthly business functions. He decided to schedule backwards and to increase his contacts with more efficient scheduling!

Lesson #2: It's not who you know, but who THEY know!

Lesson #3: Schedule backwards!

It's The Little Things That Win
And Keep Customers

I have one of those old round thermostats in my house. One day the circular plastic cover fell off and one of my children threw it away. So, I had a thermostat without a plastic cover. Apparently, no hardware store in the world carried that part, but I did not want to buy a whole new thermostat just for the plastic cover.

I proceeded to contact a few different heating and air conditioning companies. I even stopped in at a few of them, explained my situation, left my business card and asked if they could save a plastic cover when they replaced an old round thermostat. At each of these businesses the owners/workers said that they run across these types of thermostats all the time. They all said they would be more than glad to save a plastic cover for me. It took over a year before a company actually saved me a plastic cover. Guess who got all my company's heating and air conditioning business from that day on? And guess who received thousands of dollars of referrals from me for heating and air conditioning work?

It appears that many businesses are only *big job oriented*. This attitude will silently and significantly decrease both your current and future growth. It is a well known fact that most customers who leave their current suppliers or service contractors never tell them why. Many times you lose customers because of the little things that you fail to do or respond to. Remember, if you don't want to do the little things, your competitors will be eager to take your place. Customers don't just want to be serviced — they want to be *pampered*.

I take advantage of every opportunity I have to provide a little extra service to my customers. It could be something as simple as mailing copies of an interesting article or legal decision that may affect their business. On several occasions I mailed the original of an article that was written about my clients. I congratulated them

15

on the article and let them know I thought they might want the extra enclosed article. I am amazed at the response I get from this simple gesture.

Another technique that I utilize is to provide some short information seminars on pertinent and current topics that I think would interest my clients. I save them both money and potential future problems.

There are many little opportunities to show your regular customers that you care. If you are one of the businesses that think it doesn't make a difference, just ask your customers. *Remember: out of sight, out of mind!*

Lesson #4: It's the little things that win and keep customers.

Lesson #5: Don't be just a big job oriented company or service.

Lesson #6: Customers don't just want to be serviced — they want to be pampered.

Lesson #7: Remember: out of sight, out of mind!

The Two Most Important Words In Business

Thank You! I think these two simple words have become extinct in our daily lives, both in personal and business usage. I have to give credit to my wife, Michelle, for her help in this area. She really stressed to me the importance of responding with **WRITTEN** thank you cards from Day One of our marriage. I sent thank you cards, but not to the degree she insisted. But she was right on the money with this attitude. A thank you does more than just let the person know you appreciate their generosity. It also lets them know you actually received their gift or referral. Many times you wonder if the person got it in the mail, if the shipment reached them or if the referral made contact with them.

In the business world this area of etiquette is rapidly becoming extinct. If you want to have an edge on the competition a simple *acknowledgment system* will provide you with a distinct advantage. Business referral (i.e. networking) is a more prevalent aspect of business today than ever before. How can you expect continued referrals when you consistently consider acknowledging the business referral as a minor issue? An acknowledgment system is a very integral aspect of business development and growth.

I *personally* send a thank you card for every known referral I receive. I'll repeat what you just read: I *personally* — not my secretary — send a thank you card for every known referral I receive. Why? I receive a tremendous number of referrals and it grows every week, month and year. I attribute the vast majority of this referral growth to my written appreciation system. It only takes a few minutes to send a card. I always buy four to six different types of thank you cards so that I have a variety to send to the same person.

I have had business associates call me and say, "Tim, you don't have to send me any more thank you notes. I'll keep sending you referrals because you do a great job." I respond to them that I appreciate the call, but I never want them to think I expect referrals without acknowledgment. I also explain this is a way they know their referral actually reached me in case they talk to that referral again. I keep sending the thank you cards because once again, *out of sight, out of mind!*

The Cleveland Indians built a new baseball stadium, Gateway, in downtown Cleveland. We also have the Cleveland Browns Stadium at another downtown location. Going to the baseball stadium is very different from going to the Cleveland Browns Stadium. At the baseball stadium, as you walk through the gates, an employee thanks you for coming to the stadium. If you bring a group to visit the game you receive a nice thank you letter after your visit. Those types of things are nonexistent at the football stadium. Why? The new baseball stadium management trained all employees on etiquette techniques. I have had numerous people comment on the appreciation of the baseball employees. Will they get a return for their acknowledgment system? You can bet on it!

One last comment on sending thank you letters and cards. Since customers assume your secretary may have typed the thank you letter, a *hand-written* thank you card is always viewed as more personal and definitely coming from you. For these specific reasons I no longer send thank you *letters* — and the results have been very favorable.

If you still desire to use the thank you letter that is your choice. The letter will be appreciated, but you can do two things to improve its use. First, write a simple note at the bottom in your handwriting, such as "P.S. Call me for lunch" or "Say hello to the family for me," etc. Second, sign all letters in **BLUE INK**. Black ink can appear like a stamp, but blue indicates that you took the time to sign the letter for sure.

Lesson #8: The two most important words in business are "thank you."

Lesson #9: An acknowledgment system utilizing a thank you in writing is very important in business.

Lesson #10: Always sign your name in blue ink.

Don't Forget Your ROOTS

Many successful people in all areas of life forget their roots. This upsets me and I know that it upsets the forgotten also. Nobody succeeds *on their own*! Everyone has parents/family who spent unlimited time, money and energy on raising, molding and guiding the winners. Everyone has friends, associates, and business contacts who made a significant difference in the direction and level of success you have achieved or will achieve. Finally, these key people and the new relationships developed will make a significant difference in your continued future success!

I distinctly remember several key support and influential people from when I started my business. First was my parents. Both of their families were based with strong work ethics that were definitely passed along to my parents and instilled in me. My parents accepted nothing but doing it the right way and always supported me with "a you are your only limit" attitude. They instilled strong confidence in me, which gave me the ability to take on any task and succeed!

Second, I married into a great family. My father-in-law and mother-in-law have both been extremely supportive of my business goals. They always want to share in the excitement, disappointments and discussions of the company's future. I had my company for just two years when I needed to buy my own building and build a much larger and more diverse company under one roof. The banks would not finance the building acquisition due to the short track record of my company, even though the record was strong, with good profits. My in-laws provided a large cash down payment for the purchase of the building. When you take into consideration the fact that that they worked their entire lives and now had enough confidence to place a significant part of their life's effort in my hands, you see why I have nothing but admiration and gratitude for them!

Everyone who succeeds has at least one or two outside influences that support their success in one way or another. I relied on one significant and influential person who owned a retail store. His name was Frank Klansek. Before I started my own company I would discuss it with Frank who, as a business owner, clearly understood the basics of business. We would talk for hours on end about how to build a successful business. But, more importantly, he would consistently tell me that I was a winner, that I would succeed, that I had what few others possessed to be a winner. He always talked about positive attitude. He always extended my company unlimited credit for supplies. He didn't do this just because he was a nice person, but because he had full confidence in me. I made sure that I never forgot all of his different forms of support. I have sent him continuous business and, when I expanded into the uniform security business, who do you think was awarded the contract to supply all the uniforms, equipment and accessories to support that new division? Additionally, Frank and I have breakfast together approximately once every two months. I never want to forget this "root" and as long as I am alive I won't. I'll never be so big or so successful that I won't have time for him or my family who supported me when I was a nobody!

The fourth area of influence which contributed to my success was several key business associates. These are the other business professionals with whom you develop relationships as you build your business. At the beginning of my business career I had contact with business associates from both small and large corporations. Some of the key corporate executives from larger companies wanted nothing to do with the "little guy." Others were very interested and supportive. I haven't forgotten who was supportive *before* I developed a national reputation and a much larger corporation. I also remember those individuals who didn't have the time of day for me at the beginning. All of a sudden, now that I am successful, I am apparently worthy of their acknowledgment and conversation.

The last and most important "root" to *never* forget is your immediate family. Surveys and examination of successful business people in the past and present have revealed that the majority of successful business people are happily married and supported by their spouses. I feel there is no stronger key element in the success of any business person than their spouse's support.

In my case, my wife, Michelle, has been a consistent source of support while we suffered through the rough monetary times. When we first bought the building, Michelle and our three children cleaned it every week, mowed the grass and took on other tasks for the new business that we could not afford to contract out. Michelle never condemned me when money was short and we had to use charge cards to make payroll and pay bills. Most of all, she always ended our joyful and concerned conversations with, "Tim, I know that you will always find the way to make the business and your family a success!" That kind of support always made me begin the next business morning with a smile on my face, confidence in my heart and determination to succeed in my soul!

In 1996 I was awarded the prestigous "Small Business Entrepreneur of the Year" award by the Akron Regional Development Small Business Council. The night of the award presentation I had to give an acceptance speech. Part of it focused on my personal acknowledgement and appreciation of my family, business peers and employees in supporting me through the years, which resulted in this highly regarded award.

I stressed in my acceptance speech that this award could not be accepted by me, but must be accepted by all of those who made the award possible — *my roots*!

The most important part of my acceptance speech was when I acknowledged my wife's efforts through all the years, including the difficult ones. I presented her with a gold bracelet as a symbol of my appreciation for her steadfast dedication. The awards night just happened to be the eve of our 15th wedding anniversary. You could hear a pin drop during this part of the presentation. I was pleased to make this my wife's special night!

Lesson #11: Never, never, never forget your roots!

The "Bingo Theory" Is True

My mother has a theory I call the "bingo theory." Every time she wins at playing bingo she firmly believes in giving part of those winnings to those she loves. She always gives my three children, my wife and me a portion of her winnings. She also sends money to my brother and his family in North Carolina, even though she is in Ohio. She believes that if she gives part of what she wins, she will win more in her future bingo participation. She also believes everyone should give back to their community. For years I thought her generosity was very nice, but not necessary.

But, as I started to pay attention to her winnings record I soon discovered that she wins a lot of money at these bingo games. No longer was it just a kind gesture. I finally realized that for some unknown, "mystical" reason her bingo theory was absolutely true!

How does this apply to the business world? It's simple: you need to give back to your community on all levels in order to continue to benefit in the future. I also firmly believe everyone needs to develop a sense of personal commitment and a way to give a contribution *back* to society — and the business community is no exception.

I have become very active in various business and professional organizations. These groups have allowed me to develop a very large and extensive business contact group. These contacts go beyond the networking level, although networking is very important, as I will discuss it in a later chapter in this book.

You need to give back to the business community in some fashion that may not necessarily benefit you directly. I have chosen to never be too busy or too successful not to have time to assist other new businesses or new business professionals with my time and knowledge. I feel that I have the ability to guide them through the numerous obstacles they may encounter and save them time, aggravation and money. Hopefully I can make a difference and contribute to the success of their business dreams. Rarely does a month go by that I don't lend someone my time, ear or advice. Working with others on a regular basis keeps me sharp and humble and reminds me of my roots and how I got where I am today.

I feel no greater joy than being able to assist newer businesses with their business goals. I have had several entrepreneurs ask for my assistance and they were shocked when I said yes. I could not believe their reaction and asked them why they thought I would not be receptive to their requests. All of them said that I was successful and they felt they might be wasting my time. My response was: there is no greater joy than being part of another's success story!

Many employees in business feel guarded about training someone to be able to completely do their job. They feel if they train someone to do their job they will be replaced by the new kid on the block. This is not true. On the other hand, how can you be promoted if there is a strong need for your specific job and no one is ready to assume your duties?

I am constantly asked to provide presentations for church groups, parent groups, students, civic groups, etc. These groups have no money, but hearts of gold. In my opinion they are the backbone of our local communities. I provide numerous presentations yearly to these groups and my payment is the attentiveness and sincere appreciation that these individuals and groups express to me. It would be easy to say no (and many times I have been extremely busy or tired), but each time I finish I know that God has asked me to give back just a little effort! If I make a difference for just one person at those presentations then I am satisfied. Everyone must dedicate themselves to giving back in some fashion a little bit of their God-given talent. An additional positive result of this attitude is that it will keep you in touch with the people in your community. This will benefit you considerably in your day-to-day business environment. Many successful people become less successful because they are lacking in this important area.

Ironically, some great friendships have developed from the business goals that I have established for myself. I will also admit that some great benefits have developed out of these new relationships, even though that was not my original intention.

Finally, this attitude keeps you in touch with the "front line" of the businesses. If you do not think this is important remember that over 80% of the businesses that exist in the United States are classified as "small businesses."

Lesson #12: Remember the "bingo theory."

Lesson #13: Be a contributing participant of someone else's success.

Make Your Client Contact
Look Good First

Dave Nicholson and I were referred to a company to provide some training on one of our nationally copyrighted management training programs. This large, national company, based in Cleveland, was very anxious to receive (and in need of) this training. At the same time, they were going through some major restructuring, including the changing of their top executive. This company had recently suffered certain financial declines and was the subject of several business articles. Needless to say, the pressure was on our contacts with this company to make the correct management and financial decisions.

After a few months of careful relationship building we came to an agreement to provide a training program for all of their management. During the first management training session, we noticed that the two personal contacts with whom we had arranged the management training were noticeably nervous. After we got through the first hour of training, the contacts' nervousness began to diminish a little. When we finally finished our first training for this company's management, our contacts had smiles on their faces and their nervousness had completely disappeared.

When Dave and I talked to them after the first management training session they said something very interesting. They apologized for being outwardly nervous, explaining that the company was obviously going through some difficult times, both financially and structurally. Best of all, they informed us that their company had *never* utilized outside consultants for any type of management training. They further explained that they both felt their personal reputation was on the line with their employer. They had sold their national company on our training program. Little did we know the magnitude of their decision.

We made these two key management personnel look good. We have returned to their company for several additional training sessions. They believe in us and we benefit from their strong reference and the lasting relationship we have developed. It all started with our delivering what we promised and making the key people look good!

Many business professionals focus on how their business deals make them and their company look good. This is fine, but should be secondary to making your client contact(s) look good. Why? If the business contact with whom you have established a relationship comes out of the deal smelling like a rose, he/she will never want to end his or her relationship with you. In fact, that contact is going to desire to continue working with you for years to come. The new business customer will also request additional services you can provide for one simple reason — you and your service will continue to make them look good!

With the constant downsizing (rightsizing, reengineering, correctsizing, etc.), professionals are often changing jobs. Today's college graduates can expect to change jobs an average of 4 to 6 times in their working lifetime. With this in mind, remember that if you were a proven winner who created positive results and made someone look good at his or her previous job, he or she will seek you out on the next employment move! I have experienced this several times. The nice thing about this situation is that the original company will continue to utilize your services. This is because you have become a familiar service provider and have established a solid relationship with several key management personnel. When a key contact leaves a company where you have built a relationship, you need to find that key person's replacement. You then have to build a strong new relationship with the replacement and **once again** make them look good on a regular basis.

Keep in mind that the old contact you had developed a strong relationship with will most likely be working for another company. Down the road chances are strong that you may get another call from this contact who now represents another company. This actually happened to me. When the gentleman contacted me I was at first confused, since I didn't even know that he had left the other company. But the first thing he said to me was that for a long time he had wanted to utilize my services with the other company, but kept getting denied his request. He further stated he was excited that his current company was very positive about using my services, based on his recommendation.

There are two other simple techniques to help your business contacts look good. First, make sure your key contact(s) understand clearly that you want them to contact you by phone for questions and advice anytime they need help. Second, make sure your key contact(s) clearly understand that you will *not* charge them for simple advice over the phone. This may seem simple and obvious to you, but many company contacts are apprehensive about calling and unsure if they will be charged. (Once again, if you are a consistent supporter they will always look good and won't forget who helped them get there.) Some people in business may disagree with this and think that they will be taken advantage of. In my experience this has not happened. I have been using this system for over five years without any problems and I have never been taken advantage of. If the contact needs extensive assistance they have always told me that their needs are not simple, that we need to meet, and that they would be more than willing to pay for my expertise and guidance. These key contacts remember all the times we assisted for no fee. They don't want to take advantage of you because they don't want to lose your support! Finally, any time the assistance requested over the phone becomes extensive, I have never experienced a negative reaction from informing the client that my assistance in this specific situation will require monetary compensation.

The other simple way to build your strong relationship with companies and key contacts is by using a unique billing system that I practice. If I provide a free service that I often charge for I will send a regular billing listing the customary charges. The next line on the billing states your customer appreciation discount is equal to the billing rate so that the total amount charged is ZERO! The key contact is sent this billing. What do you think that person does with this billing? They show it to their boss for three reasons. The first reason is to make themselves look good. They have bragging rights to clearly show they saved the company money while solving a company problem. Second, they are also making *you* look good with their boss since they want you to stay on their support team. Third, they are going to be able to convince their boss to utilize you in the future for additional services since you don't require compensation for every little service you provide!

Professional people do business with people who they have developed a *relationship* with and who *appreciate* each other's efforts! This attitude builds lasting relationships. Or, you can choose the attitude of those who believe they don't have the time for these little efforts, and thus *limit your growth.*

Lesson #14:   Make your client contact look good first.

Lesson #15:   Encourage simple phone advice at no charge.

Lesson #16:   Send zero amount billings for free service that normally is billed.

Lesson #17:   Professional people do business with people who they have developed a relationship with and who appreciate each other's efforts.

Trust Your Gut Instincts

When I worked as an undercover narcotics officer there were several occasions where "gut instinct" made a big difference. In fact, I may not have been here today writing this book without the use of my gut instinct in my law enforcement career.

This gut instinct is no different in the day-to-day business world. I have had several occasions where I was engaged in formulating a business relationship, price quotation, etc. but didn't feel comfortable with the situation. I felt I was being led down some unknown path, with me taking all the chances and contributing the majority of time, money and/or effort.

You have to examine the little things that your business contacts promise to follow through with. Many times this can tell you the level of sincerity of the person involved. See if they are willing to do things without payment. See if they are willing to carry some of the load. See if they have initiative or if it is always your initiative and effort that is involved.

I was involved in a business deal at one time that started out on a very strong footing. The first few months I made strong sales and profits. But several months later the competition started to catch on to the reasons for our success. I sensed what was starting to transpire and wanted to make some adjustments to the business strategy. I could not convince the other business entities involved of the need to change our strategy. At the same time, I had a significant amount of money invested. More importantly, I had a tremendous amount of time invested into what I knew could be a winner. I had convinced other business people to get involved.

I had to make a hard decision that was based mostly on my "gut feelings." It was a tough decision, but I decided to follow my instinct and pull out of this business relationship, in which I was a key player. I decided to be upfront with my decision and explain to everyone my discomfort with the situation. I decided that no more money and time would be spent on this business venture — and this decision was based on my "gut feelings." A year later my gut feelings proved accurate, as I witnessed the total collapse of the business entity involved.

A side note on this type of business situation: The hardest business deals to get out of are the ones in which you already have money and/or time invested. This situation can result in more money being invested after the original money has resulted in a low return. The additional money is invested in hopes of salvaging the original investment. This pattern can continue to repeat itself several times as you sink deeper and deeper. When this is taking place you need the ability to stop early and keep your losses to a minimum.

The simple solution to this type of business trap is to set specific result goals for your investment and/or involvement. If these goals are not achieved, have a specific plan to avoid continuing in your unproductive direction.

If for some reason it doesn't "feel right" you are probably better to follow your "gut instinct." Many important business decisions have been made based purely on gut feelings. Many of these decisions were made accurately and for the best of all parties involved.

Lesson #18: Trust your gut instincts.

Lesson #19: Many important business decisions have been made purely based on gut feelings.

Lesson #20: If it doesn't "feel right" don't do it!

Separate Yourself From The Rest

This is easier said than done. There are so many ways you can separate yourself from the rest. First you start with the service/product that you offer. Second, examine the routine support that you provide the customer.

I was in Cleveland, Ohio at a COSE (Council of Smaller Enterprises) breakfast meeting which featured both a networking opportunity and an informative speaker. Similar to many other small business meetings, the forum gave everyone an opportunity to briefly explain their business to all the participants present. I had the opportunity to do this before on many occasions, generating a modest amount of interest. This time I stood and explained that my company provides management training and human resource assistance. I then said, "My company puts you back in control." If you want to know more see me after the presentation." I had a line of people who wanted to talk with me, get my business card and meet with me later. Why? I said something very unique that hit home with these business professionals. It was something they felt they haven't been able to get from anyone else! I had hit the soul of their business needs. I have since developed my company to provide unique services that I explain are not obtainable anywhere else. I developed my "unique niche" in the market!

I've worked with a professional marketing company, Walder Communications, over the years. Kathleen Walder and her staff have had a tremendous impact in assisting my company to get noticed. Kathleen has shown me how to get free news coverage and, more importantly, how to get the news media to notice you. She has always supported my contention that "you must separate yourself from the rest."

Kathleen does a great job with her newsletter titled, *"Imageination."* Her tagline is "Marketing ideas to improve your image and increase your visibility." I read with interest an advertisement she published on her company. It said if you've seen Walder Communications folks out and about recently, you "probably noticed our feet—actually our feet stickers." The feet help us explain what Walder Communication does. Kathleen further explains that public relations is difficult to explain in a word. "So, we say we deal in feet. We either help you put your best foot forward, or we help you keep your foot out of your mouth." Who would ever forget what Walder Communications does if they read that memorable little tidbit?

How about those people at Blockbuster Video? A new one opened by my residence. When I walked in the door the young man at the counter said, "Hello." I was slightly surprised and thought it was just by chance. I stood back and observed him saying hello to everyone who walked in that door. That simple gesture made me feel special. Also, they notice your name on the Blockbuster card and thank you by name. What a nice touch. People do like to hear their name. It's a great marketing and personalization tool!

When asked who my competition is, I state that my programs are so unique that I have no competition. There may be some businesses providing some programs with similar names, but I explain with confidence that the presentation I provide cannot be matched. I explain that my unique background and understanding of the topic separates me from the others. You have to make sure that you explain your services with confidence and not with your ego.

Routine support comes in many forms, but none is more important than the return of phone calls. If I have one main complaint it is the abuse of the phone system by professionals. I have a golden rule at my company. Return *all* phone calls within 24 hours. I explain to my employees that they must return all phone calls within 24 hours and that includes the calls to people you don't like, don't want to talk to or have no idea why they called. I explain to my employees that if they don't like the person who called, call back and tell them you don't like them, but return the call.

When I am out of town I make sure that my staff knows when I will return. I ask my secretary to clearly explain that I won't be back until a specific date. If the client wasn't told I was out of town then my secretary calls the client to let them know I am out of town. If I have time while out of town I call in for messages. If time permits, I call the client, inform them I am out of town, called in for messages and thought I would check with them to make sure it wasn't a pressing issue. My clients are very appreciative of my extra effort and concern. They usually let me know what they wanted and that it wasn't pressing. When I get back to my office I already know what they need, promptly address their needs and, in so doing, separate my service from the rest. Do you think those clients inform other business professionals of my extra effort? What's the competition doing in the same situation? If I didn't have time to call them while I was out of town, the client often lets me know they really appreciated being informed by my secretary that I was out of town and when I will return.

I had to make a decision on whether to expand my phone system into a larger electronic answering system or hire another person to answer the phones. I chose the latter and have had tremendous response from clients. One of the compliments I hear most often about my company is that we have "human beings" answering the phone and "they are very pleasant." This helps separate my company from many others.

Voice mail is a great business tool. Unfortunately, many professionals abuse this system on a regular basis. Voice mail was originally invented as a communication tool, not a filtering system. If you are utilizing voice mail as a filtering system it will come back to haunt you in the long run. Business professionals will discuss their displeasure with other professionals who abuse this system.

I have encountered voice mail abuse a few times, just as everyone else has. I have developed a simple solution to combat this abuse. First, you leave a few messages on the person's voice mail noting the contact person, times and dates in that specific business file. After a couple attempts with no returned call you send a very simple letter. In the letter explain all the times and dates you made the calls, explain that your time is very important and that you would appreciate a short return call even if there is no interest, so that you can clear your files. When most professionals see, *in writing*, their reputation on the line they will do whatever it takes to clear their reputation. Once you send the letter they can't hide behind the invisible and impersonal voice mail. Your letter is a mirror that they must look through.

There are many methods to separate yourself from the rest. Most of them are ingrained in traditional business methods that your parents and grandparents utilized. Examine your day-to-day business activity and look for opportunities to separate yourself from the rest rather than running from the opportunities.

Lesson #21:   Develop a "unique niche" in the market.

Lesson #22:   Develop and have no competition.

Lesson #23:   Return all phone calls within 24 hours.

Lesson #24:   Don't abuse the "voice mail" systems.

Lesson #25:   Examine your day-to-day business activity and look for the opportunity to separate yourself from the rest and not the chance to ignore the opportunity.

Networking = Relationship Building?

One of the most misunderstood business terms commonly used is the term "networking." You will see business organizations constantly profess the opportunity for business professionals to network at their upcoming function.

Many professionals envision this networking opportunity as a chance to expand their business by meeting new potential clients and telling them all about their services. Who wants to do business with someone they don't know personally first? Who wants to do business with someone who has no interest in learning about them first? Finally, who wants to do business with someone who wants to take, take, and take without giving, giving and giving?

Networking needs to be viewed as "relationship building." How do you build a relationship, whether it is personal or business? First, you get to know the person. Ask about their interests, hobbies, family, etc. You may find you have some common interests or friends. Second, find out about their company, services/products and the person's role in the company. Third, find out what their company goals/needs are. Finally, discuss what their obstacles currently are in reaching those goals/needs.

Earlier in this book I stressed that business professionals want to do business with others where a *relationship* has been established and with those who *appreciate* them! Networking opportunities establish the framework for relationship building to take place or to begin to develop. Too many professionals expect to walk out of such opportunity meetings with solid sales instead of with the beginning of a long-term relationship that will result in future business and several additional referrals.

Second, in many cases some professionals you meet at a networking opportunity appear to have no value to you since they won't be able to utilize your service. Most professionals who experience this situation move on to the next potential candidate. What a crucial mistake! *Everyone* is a very important client to your business. Why? Because everyone knows numerous other business professionals, they have family and friends involved in other businesses that may need your services, and they can spread your name in a positive or negative fashion. It is not only important who *you* know, but also important who *they* know!

What other networking methods can be very effective in building relationships? One that I have had tremendous success with is joining professional business groups such as chambers, rotary, professional organizations, etc. Not only should you join these groups, but you should be involved on a committee within these groups. You will build strong relationships which will definitely result in additional business. I have utilized this aspect of networking to its fullest. Personally, I think this is the best networking opportunity and relationship building method I have found. The results for me have been tremendous!

A very good friend and business associate of mine by the name of Roy Wilson is known for his knowledge and abilities in the networking field. He actually has a registered name of "Mr. Network." He has a business card printed with his definition of what networking truly should be. With his permission I have included his definition:

Networking is about establishing relationships — people helping people. Networking is not about business but rather sharing with others our knowledge and experience about who we are and what we do. Networking is about intelligent beings helping other human beings to become successful in life, health and business, whatever their definitions of success may be, because a networker understands that by helping others find their way, we insure our own future success. A networker studies, learns and practices the philosophy, principles and concepts of networking and teaches others through mentoring and personally setting an example for others to follow. Resolve today to become a true networker by giving of yourself to the service of others and enhance your life, health and business through networking!

A NETWORKER...

A= Always has a great attitude

N= Never speaks ill of another human being, is
E= Enthusiastic, positive and motivated, a
T= Teamplayer working for the success of others, a
W= Winner, never a loser but is
O= Observant for opportunities and
R= Respectful of others and is
K= Kind to all mankind while
E= Empathic to others' problems and always
R= Reliable- *their word is their bond*!

When I became involved in several business organizations I immediately realized the value of networking. Sadly, over time, the term "networking" has become tarnished, overused, and in many instances, has actually developed a negative connotation. I have also experienced on numerous occasions how professional business associates have abused and/or misunderstood their proper role in a networking environment.

I set out to create a new term that I felt would more accurately describe what should take place at business functions that were previously listed under the "networking" banner. Since my true belief in business is that we need to build relationships, both personally and on a business level, I have created a new word that I feel more accurately focuses on that goal.

The new term that I developed is "businesships." This is the system of building both a personal and business relationship with your clients and suppliers to your business. Obviously, there will be varying degrees of this relationship. Some relationships will be quite close and others will not be as close. But all of them should focus on getting to know business contacts more than just by name or only for your personal benefit or gain. Businesships build relationships — and relationships build a solid business!

Lesson #26: Networking needs to be viewed as "relationship building."

Lesson #27: Building a relationship means:
1.) Getting to know them
2.) Getting to know their company
3.) Getting to know their goals/needs
4.) Getting to know their obstacles

Lesson #28: It is not only important who *you* know, but also who *they* know.

Lesson #29: Network by joining professional organizations and getting involved on their committees.

Lesson #30: Businesships build relationships and relationships build a solid business.

When Do You Know You're Really Good?

Early in my career, I met a gentleman after a brief business presentation that I gave at a local business luncheon. He was a businessman in charge of operations at a country club. He informed me he was impressed with my knowledge and presentation skills. He asked me to meet with him to provide a quote on some management training services he desired for his business.

I met with him and quite a large group of managers and other business associates who wanted me to provide this specific training program I had developed into a nationally copyrighted program. My original price was $1,200 for a session. He called me back a week later and wanted to know if I could reduce my price a bit to fit his budget. After I asked him a few more questions I was able to adjust my price a few hundred dollars. He said that he would call me back.

Approximately ten days later I received a phone call from this man's secretary. She said that her boss, Mr. X, had asked her to call me. She was to inform me that Mr. X could not pay the fee I quoted him and wanted to know if I would do the training program for $500. I was shocked, angry and disappointed all at the same time.

It took me a few moments of silence to catch my mental thoughts. I also debated if I wanted to turn down $500 for a day's training. I certainly could use that money — and what about all those people I wouldn't be exposed to for future business opportunities if I chose not to do it?

I then remembered what a nationally recognized speaker/trainer had told me at a business meeting. She told me, "Tim, you know you're good and you have reached another level when you can turn down business."

I kindly informed the secretary that my time and expertise did not permit me to provide that level of service for the nominal fee of $500. I appreciated their interest, but would have to decline.

I got off the phone still questioning in my heart and soul whether I had done the correct thing. Then I kept repeating in my mind what that expert had said. As I kept repeating her words I felt stronger and stronger and stronger in my conviction that I had indeed done the right thing. I also remembered her other words of advice. She said, "When you allow one client to beat you down in price, they have bragging rights and they will let the world know you can be obtained at a greatly reduced rate. Just think of all the money you lose by giving everyone significantly reduced rates on a regular basis." Her final comment never leaves my mind. "You can *never* buy a Cadillac at a Ford price."

By the day's end I was flying high as a kite. I was so excited that I was calling myself "Mr. Cadillac." I knew that I had met one of the most crucial internal challenges of my business career and I felt good about the results. It was definitely a personal confidence builder that I will never forget. I had risen one more level on the professional business career track. This accomplishment was due to the wisdom of another business associate who had been there before and took the time to share with me a vital lesson in the business world.

Lesson #31: You know you're good and you have reached another level when you can turn down business.

Lesson #32: When you allow one client to beat you down in price too much, they have bragging rights and they will let the world know you can be obtained at a greatly reduced rate.

Lesson #33: You can never buy a Cadillac at a Ford price.

I'll Never Need To Do That

When I first decided to go into business for myself I saw and met many successful people. I would talk to them and they would explain the habits they developed which helped them become successful in their business careers.

As my experience and contacts grew month by month and year by year, I would continue to hear many successful business professionals repeat the same affirmations of habit. I strongly believed that some of those business habits were not necessary for my business success. I even felt that doing things that other successful professionals did was an unnecessary waste of time.

Little by little, I found out that my resistance was only delaying my growth and success. I finally reached a point where I would seek out all the little things and habits that successful people exemplified and I began experimenting with them in my daily business routine. I started to see a pattern. The more successful I am is directly related to how I utilize the habits of other successful business people locally and nationally.

There isn't some specific reason for the success of one business versus the failure of another. It is a simple and well known fact that if you want to become successful, you must study and copy the business habits of those who are already successful. Simply put: "Don't reinvent the wheel." Millions of business professionals have already experienced trial and error. Save your time and energy by trying the methods that have already worked for the cream of the crop in business currently and in the past!

I can't believe how closed-minded I was when I first started. I didn't think image was a major issue. I didn't think wearing a coat and tie would make a difference. I found out I was dead wrong! I didn't think that wearing a sharp, well tailored suit with a nice shirt and tie mattered. I found out I was wrong. Once I realized this, and changed, I noticed that, when I walked in the room, people noticed me first (instead of the other guy), because I dressed with style and confidence.

I never liked to read much. I read regularly now. I read business books, sales books, marketing books, success books, several newspapers, magazines, etc. Why? Successful people kept telling me to stay in tune with the business environment nationally and internationally. As I read more and more, I discovered business trends that I needed to adjust for and/or prepare for — in many cases months before my competition even dreamed of the coming changes. I became better versed in my conversations, speeches and presentations. Other business associates wanted to know how I knew this piece of vital information. Other businesses would seek me out for advice and direction. It increased my credibility and my hourly billing fees. I was increasing my fees and having an easier time obtaining these higher fees. Why? Because I did what other successful business associates did.

Several years ago I swore that one thing I would never be interested in doing was listening to cassette tapes in my car. I thought this was stupid and a waste of time. I thought cassettes were on the way out. Did I predict that accurately? No. Business information and training cassettes are a huge market today! I am always listening to cassettes in my car. Driving time is a waste of time if you are not listening to cassettes. You can learn and review so much crucial business material with cassettes while you are driving. Ironically, I am in the process of signing an agreement to put my training programs on cassettes.

I could go on but there is a list of other common habits and traits of successful people that you can read in numerous success books, see on success videos and hear about in your car on cassettes.

Lesson #34: If you want to become successful study and copy the business habits of those who are already successful.

Lesson #35: Don't reinvent the wheel.

Lesson #36: Read, read and read more.

Lesson #37: Listen to cassettes in your car and gain an edge.

If You're Not Part Of The Success, You May Be Part Of The Failure

I had an early morning breakfast with a close business associate who wanted to review his current business growth plan with me. He explained that he didn't feel that he was getting his message out and therefore his business was suffering.

My first question to him was: do you want to increase your business? He naturally replied, "Yes! Definitely!" I then asked him how many potential clients he got to meet on a weekly basis. His reply to this specific question was not impressive. At this point I knew that we needed to examine more closely why his weekly contact numbers were low. It was clear to me this business friend was not *meeting people, meeting people, meeting people*!

I asked if he belonged to any professional organizations. He said he belonged to a few. I asked if he was a board member or officer on any of them. He said no! I stopped him there and said, "How do you expect people to visualize you and/or your business as a 'cut above' your competition when you have never taken the opportunity to clearly exemplify that 'aura'?" He really didn't understand what I was attempting to explain.

I explained that business people want to be associated with "leaders in the community." The leaders rise from professional organizations, articles are written about these individuals, their businesses and their success. Other businesses perceive that these specific individuals and their businesses must be very successful and among the best in their industry. Then what happens? These business associates seek out you and your business first. You make a strong impression and they will think of you first when the need arises. Also, they will suggest you first when others inquire about a provider of that specific service. I cannot tell you how many direct and indirect referrals I have obtained from this exact situation. (I sent a thank you to every single referral also.)

How do you obtain this level of contact? You not only join the professional organizations, but you become active in them. Immediately, everyone thinks: "I don't have the time." I say you can't afford *not* to have the time. Get rid of other little projects that don't get you face-to-face with potential clients. Many of these groups don't ask for a great deal of time. Become part of the "success team!" Many professional organizations need business people only for special yearly projects. Be part of their board, head up a committee, become active and you will *meet people, meet people and meet people.* The end result will be more leads, more business, more friendships and more enjoyment for you. This whole chapter aligns itself with the chapter on "separating yourself from the rest." If you want more business you have to separate yourself from the rest and you have to *become active.* I can summarize this whole chapter in one simple sentence: *Out of sight — out of mind!*

Let me complete this chapter with a few other insights on joining professional groups. First, don't join a professional group and do all the work. This is an easy trap to fall in to. Join with the intention to do your part. If you find yourself doing more and more you need to get out of that group. You could end up doing more work for that professional group than for your own business. Always monitor your time to make sure that this never happens. If you see this type of activity you need to make your observations known and request assistance. If no one steps forward to assist, then step down from that position at the end of your term. Find other professional groups that do not function that way. Don't think you can change the group by your individual efforts. You might be able to, but the amount of time and effort is not worth it and you should not have to accomplish such an enormous task by yourself.

The second area of advice is: surround yourself with other workers and doers! You know who in the business community is a "worker" or a "doer." Go to them and seek their participation and support! Many times you will find that they are very receptive to your request, especially if they know you are part of the team or leading the team. They will also ask you who else is part of the team. Why? Because many of these special people have been "abused" in the past by other professional organizations and they

50

have learned. Workers and doers like being around workers and doers. The people you recruit then have a sense of confidence that their time and effort won't be abused, they will enjoy the participation and they will be part of a successful effort.

Third, never, never, *never* forget to give credit to your committee members. If you are in charge of a professional group or are a committee chairman, make sure you provide regular and individual positive feedback to your support group. A simple acknowledgment of thanks is all most people need to maintain that fire burning — to continue supporting your group's efforts.

I belonged to a professional organization where I was very active. For four years I kept repeating that we needed more participation on the board and with the committees. The following year I decided to become chairman. I was elected chairman and also chaired the program committee. I was permitted and expected to provide leadership, do most of the work and arrange the majority of the monthly speakers. I found out quickly that my time was being abused. It got to the point where I couldn't wait for the end of the year. I quietly declined any further position at all. I will attend these meetings only if no other opportunity arises. The worst part of this situation was that I didn't enjoy going to these functions anymore. When you cease having fun it becomes painful! The ironic twist is that this group is made up of some really good friends and successful business associates, but they lack the motivation to take the group to a higher level. They are content with a minimal effort. I refused to be part of this minimal effort.

I should have seen the writing on the wall three years ago with this particular group. I thought my efforts could bring them out of the hole, but I also found out they have to desire the same goal and provide the support and effort. They were not willing to pay the price so I had to make the decision that was best for me.

I am involved with The Akron Regional Development Board and The Small Business Council, two of the larger professional groups in the three-county area. I am both a board member and a team member on the program committee. Jerry Kostelny was chairman of the program committee and was my mentor. He was professional in everything that he did. This group had some obstacles to overcome and slowly, under Jerry's leadership, we progressed. Basically, our group was responsible for a monthly breakfast series which included a presentation by a speaker on specific topics pertaining to small business. With Jerry's leadership and the group's effort we were able to eliminate several obstacles and move the monthly breakfast series forward with the result being a more positive image.

Jerry and I had worked very closely together to organize this very important committee. He decided to move on with his business goals and I became chairman of the program committee. I decided to make additional changes in both the members of this committee and the actual structure of the monthly breakfast series.

The first change I sought was to include members on this committee representing all three counties that were marketed under the flag of the Akron Regional Development Board and Small Business Council. I felt we would attract more participation at these monthly meetings if we had more representation from those areas. We needed to develop more personal and business relationships in those areas.

Second, we changed the format of the breakfast series. We conducted surveys among the members of the Akron Regional Development Board asking why they joined this professional organization. The top two answers given were always networking and group benefits. The Akron Regional Development Board had recently put several new benefit packages together which caused a surge in membership. But, the members still wanted more and better networking opportunities.

I decided the program committee needed to do its part in the networking area. The format of the monthly breakfast series was changed to include a 10 minute networking opportunity at the start of each monthly meeting. I placed a program committee member at each table and instructed them to initiate a short networking session at their respective tables, on my cue. Each participant was to give a 30-60 second commercial on their business. We also encouraged participants to bring business cards for distribution at their tables. In addition, participants had an opportunity to mingle both before and after the formal presentation.

Our goal was to increase the attendance of this monthly breakfast series by 25%. In just three short months it increased by over 100%. I believe this was a direct result of listening to what the membership desired and making those changes, having good support team members, getting the committee members involved so that they felt part of the success, and giving those committee members credit.

This attitude goes along with two strong beliefs I have. The first is: If you help others become successful you will succeed also. The second is: If you're not part of the success you may be part of the failure!

Lesson #38: **Business people want to be associated with leaders in the community.**

Lesson #39: **Become part of a successful team in a professional organization.**

Lesson #40: **Remember: Out of sight, out of mind.**

Lesson #41: **Surround yourself with workers and doers.**

Lesson #42: **Workers and doers like being around workers and doers.**

Lesson #43: **Never, never, never forget to give credit to your committee members.**

Lesson #44: **If you help others become successful you will succeed also.**

Lesson #45: If you're not part of the success you may be part of the failure.

A Member's Guide For Murder

(How To Ensure The Death Of Your Organization)

1. Don't attend meetings. (If you do, follow rules #2 & #3.)

2. Be sure to leave before the meeting is over.

3. Next day, find fault with the officers and committees.

4. Take no part in the association's affairs.

5. Be sure to sit in the back so you can talk to a friend.

6. Get all the association will give you but give nothing in return.

7. Never ask anyone else to join.

8. Talk cooperation but never cooperate.

9. If asked to help on anything, always say you haven't time.

10. Never accept an office because it's easier to criticize than to make changes.

11. If appointed to a committee, never give any time or service.

12. Never do more than you have to. When others willingly and unselfishly use their ability to help the association along, howl that the organization is run by a clique.

Create Excitement To Create A Winner

In 1995 the Cleveland Indians won 100 games in a new stadium. They went all the way and won the American League Championship. They fell short in the World Series to the Atlanta Braves. But I have never seen more excitement in my lifetime! I also witnessed and talked to hundreds of people who were never interested in the Cleveland Indians or baseball before, but now were obsessed with the Indians and their goal of the World Series. The Cleveland Indians' goal became each person's personal goal!

Doesn't this happen in the business community also? Sure it does. When a book is written and the reviews are strong everyone wants to purchase the book and become part of the excitement. Look at how many successful motivation speakers exist. Remember the pet rock and Cabbage Patch doll crazies? What caused the excitement?

In this book I have touched on several important areas for building a successful business. All parts of building a business are very important, but there is one aspect that I feel is of utmost importance. You need to create *excitement* in your product, your service, your employees and your clients. It doesn't have to be at the level of winning a World Series, but some form of excitement will always move your business to new heights.

Creating excitement comes in many different forms. I have seen companies and business associates use an array of methods. Remember: everyone wants to be part of the excitement. If you can create excitement, the people (and business) will follow. In an earlier chapter I discussed the increase of participants for the breakfast series. Besides the structural changes we made to the breakfast series, we also made some changes which created *excitement* for the participants to the point where they said they really looked forward to the next one and hated to miss any of the monthly functions. I would always end the function by reading some positive quotations to the participants. The participants would leave with a strong positive feeling so that they felt good about their day. How do your clients leave your business? Do they feel good and relieved or worried and distraught? I always ended the monthly function with a saying, "If you don't make the next monthly function you will be upset with yourself until the next one thirty days later!" What's the last thing you say to your customers? I tell mine I am ready to solve their problems and address their needs *immediately*! That's creating excitement! Strong growth companies don't exist without it!

Creating this kind of excitement can be contagious. If your client feels and experiences the excitement, he or she will tell several others about the excitement and become responsible for initiating the excitement. Now you have other business people desiring to be part of this excitement — which has turned into a strong momentum for your company's service and/or product.

Excitement is created simply by providing those extra small pieces of service to your clients. It is created by providing solutions to their specific needs. It is created by checking in with your customer in person or by phone for no reason at all. It is created by providing some small services and sending a bill with "no charge" listed. I could go on and on, but the idea is simply: create some excitement!

How do you get your employees excited? You have to help them experience the results of the excitement! Financial bonuses for their efforts, an extra day off, dinner for two, a simple acknowledgment of their extra effort, a thank you or an award (such as employee of the month) all are good examples of creating excitement.

One last method of creating excitement and at the same time separating yourself from the rest was introduced to me by a very close business associate of mine. Her name is Lana Thomas and her business is called GTY ("Greetings To You"). Her business specializes in sending birthday cards or other special occasion cards to your customers for you. I especially like the idea of sending birthday cards to your regular customers. Many companies send holiday cards, but I know of few businesses that send birthday cards.

This will definitely make you stand out among business associates, especially your competition.

Everyone has their own unique style. Seek advice from your own employees on how to create more excitement within your company and with your clients. I am sure you will get several good suggestions. *Be creative and the excitement will follow*!

Lesson #46: Creating excitement comes in many different forms.

Lesson #47: Remember: everyone wants to be part of the excitement.

Lesson #48: Creating excitement can be contagious for your business.

Lesson #49: Create excitement to create a winner.

Stay Focused...Stay Focused... Stay Focused!

So many times business professionals are focused at the start of their business, but soon let many other things and people get them off track. Many business professionals never regain their focus.

My good friend, Paul Sims, a training consultant associate, is president of Advanced Leadership Management Systems. He has had a tremendous influence on my business focus. I have attended several of his classes with very effective results.

Your focus should be short, simple and sweet. You should be able to summarize your focus in a very brief statement and ideally in one short sentence. I was involved in one of Paul's sales training classes and we worked on this aspect on a regular basis. We would practice our "What do you do?" statements on each other periodically. It was amazing how long and drawn out these statements were at first. I remember Brian Bowers, a salesman for Kauth Custom Builders, stating his focus was to "help people build their dreams." This person was involved in building homes. Another student, Fred Craig, was a jeweler who owned his own business. He always stated he helps people obtain "treasures you will cherish for life." Craig had an employee working for him, John Fichter, who emphasized that he "mixes elements of earth with people's desires to create smiles that last for decades." A powerful and positive statement can only enhance your business reputation.

As stated in an earlier chapter my company focus is "to put you back in control." You can provide a little more detailed explanation of your business, but you have to clearly know your focus and you have to make that same impression on your clients.

Success doesn't happen by chance except to one in a million. Success comes to those who are focused. Success starts with opportunity followed by preparation taking over! You will notice that as you become more successful you will have more people coming to you with their success ideas. Be careful whose agenda you address. It is so easy to get off your focus and even harder to get back on track once you lose your focus.

How do you become focused? Follow a business game plan. A written game plan or business plan is one of the most important aspects of a successful business! Putting your *plan* in writing is a must! It is also very important to put your *goals* in writing!

How do you plan? You need to plan carefully. Each month, day and hour needs to be planned. It has been said by several successful people that if you plan the minutes, the hours and days will take care of themselves. Paul Sims always stressed to me that the one thing you can't change in your business is the amount of time in one day — 24 hours. Therefore, Paul always stressed getting more out of the hours you work, and that comes back to planning those minutes! Organization is a cornerstone for success!

How do you organize those minutes, hours and days? If you are in business you can't do without a "time management planner." If you don't know what a planner is ask your business associates. Seriously consider taking a short training program on how to effectively utilize the planner. This is one of those things successful people do that I thought I didn't need to do. I didn't want to carry a planner around and thought I could exist without one — until I became one of the few who never had a planner with me. This caused some problems when I was working with various professional groups. Everyone was together and wanted to set up our next meeting date. Because I didn't have a planner at hand the group had to wait or set a tentative date that required several phone calls. It was quite obvious this situation took time that could have been utilized for more productive efforts. It was also obvious that I was hindering business progress for several business associates.

At my first class with Paul Sims' organization, I arrived loaded with curiosity. As I sat down at my seat I noticed a box with several items in it. One by one I took each item out of the box and found, to my surprise and pleasure, that Paul had included a "time planner" (which Paul and I now affectionately refer to as a "commitment book"). Everything in that book I am strongly committed to achieve. I now understand why everyone in business told me that they could not exist without their planners.

Focus also means that confidence in yourself must be without doubt. If you don't believe in yourself how can you expect others to believe in you? Ironically, this lack of confidence can always be seen by others. It is always sensed by other business associates. Concentrate on your strengths and never allow the thought of defeat to enter your mind. Problems will surface, but you should not let the problems distract you from total focus. Criticism, obstacles and jealous people will attempt to push and pull you off track. Once again, stay relentlessly focused.

You have to *seek* success, and your *fuel* for success is your determined mental focus! How can you hit a target (goal) if you don't have a target (goal) to hit? Once you develop a written plan for achieving your goal you need to set deadlines. Deadlines are your driving force. Deadlines also give you a barometer of your success rate.

OPPORTUNITIES never come to those who wait!

Lesson #50: **Your focus statement should be short, simple and sweet.**

Lesson #51: **You should have a written business plan and written goals.**

Lesson #52: **Success doesn't happen by chance except to one in a million.**

Lesson #53: **Success comes to those who are focused.**

Lesson #54: **Success starts with opportunity followed by preparation taking over.**

Lesson #55: Organization is the cornerstone of success.

Lesson #56: Focus also means confidence in yourself must be without doubt.

Lesson #57: If you don't believe in yourself, how can you expect others to believe in you?

Lesson #58: How can you hit a target (goal) if you don't have a target (goal) to hit?

Lesson #59: OPPORTUNITIES never come to those who wait!

Dimoff's Extra Focus Tips:

1. Focusing on your business should be your No. 1 business priority.

2. Maintain a sense of humor. Take your job seriously, but not yourself.

3. Don't dwell on the urgent and miss the important.

4. If you don't know the answer, admit it!

5. If you say you will get back to someone — don't forget!

6. Sometimes it's lonely at the top.

7. Take intelligent risks.

8. Be humble: Never ask or take credit; let it be given to you.

9. Always maintain a sense of pride and loyalty.

10. Obstacles and frustrations are part of the road to success.

11. Make good decisions about the little things.

12. Make sure your employees have their own focus and goals.

13. Make sure your employees clearly understand your *company* focus and goals.

14. Never think negatively; never let your employees think negatively.

15. Good judgment comes from experience and experience comes from bad judgment.

16. Being focused means being committed.

   To understand the difference between involvement and commitment, look at a bacon and egg breakfast. The hen is involved. The pig is committed!

How To Kill A Business

When I first entered the world of owning a business I was under the impression that "lack of customers" was the #1 reason for business failure. Even though this aspect is very important to the continued growth and success of a business, I later discovered that "lack of customers" was not the usual reason for a business to go under.

I also learned that approximately 80% of start-up businesses in the United States fail in the first five years. 80% of the remaining 20% fail in the next five years. The American Dream didn't look very positive. But, like other enthusiastic, excited business owners, I felt I could be in that small percentage who **SUCCEED** against the odds!

I started my first year working out of my basement. The second year I moved into a large health club and rented space, expanding the use of my space over the next two years while my company kept growing strongly. Then I decided to buy a building, all 8,000 square feet. I was the proud owner of a building complete with three heaters, three air conditioners, lights all over the place, money just slipping out of every window, crack, etc. In the next two years I invested over $80,000 in remodeling to make it one of the most "corporate looking" buildings in the area.

One day, the realization that I may have acquired too much, too fast started to raise its ugly head. Addtionally, the entire building was not being utilized on a daily basis. The monthly overhead was large and haunted me every month. The company was growing; we added a few new divisions, but there was still space not being utilized on a daily basis, and the monthly overhead was still knocking on the door.

As I visited other businesses that were very successful, I observed manicured cubicles for offices instead of the traditional walled offices with doors. I would observe in other businesses an area with 15-20 cubicles that in another business might have six offices. While a few of my managers were disputing who should get which office, the managers of these other companies accepted their small cubes as the norm. Companies were realizing that to survive they must do more with less, and that included less space. Basically, businesses are "maximizing their office space use" to ensure survival.

As stated before, my company grew into five divisions with close to 150 full-time/part-time employees in just five years. SACS was viewed as one of the best companies in the area. We had a great reputation that I am still very proud of. Then I experienced my next business lesson: CASH FLOW!   We had all the business we could handle and more if we wanted it. Customers were not a problem, cash for payroll was the danger area. Your employees want, need and deserve to be paid regularly and on time. I was feeling the pinch of available cash flow. Taking out a line of credit with the bank helped matters, but only to a certain degree. All the time this was going on I had a few managers and employees who couldn't understand why we were experiencing payroll demand problems. I was also becoming frustrated and strained by this problem with cash flow.

I decided to lay my company business plan and current situation on the table to several business associates that I respected. One of them was my brother, Mike, who made his living guiding businesses from start to finish.

Mike expanded our computerized accounting and tracking system so that, month-to-month, each division and every square foot of my building could be tracked to reveal the problem areas. I also diagrammed the entire SACS personnel chart to share with objective business associates for critique. (These contacts were recruited directly from my association memberships and they assisted at a "no cost fee." Who says joining these groups is a waste of time?)

The results of the tracking and the objective reviews clearly pointed out the specific problem areas and provided potential solutions. I discovered my highest paid director was overseeing the lowest profit division and, after several months of tracking this division, found it was even losing money. I decided to combine this division with another division, increasing the director's responsibility, justifying his pay and hopefully making this division profitable.

One problem with this change was that the director viewed this change as more responsibility, which deserved more pay. He really needed to view it as an opportunity to justify and keep his job. But I decided to increase his pay minimally and track the new, combined division very closely. If it failed to produce positive results I would sell it off, eliminating a big part of my business problem. Also, selling it would eliminate a large portion of my payroll cash flow demand.

Six months went by with no major results. I decided to sell the division and eliminate one director's job. But, since this director was a good organizer and was at his best when he focused on just one area, I felt he could be very valuable to a business. He just couldn't fit into the multi-faceted role that I needed. He couldn't be (and disliked being) involved in the sales and marketing end of the business — which was seriously needed in his area of responsibility.

I decided to sell that division with a few stipulations. First, I would highly recommend that the new owner keep the director and give him a fair chance. The new owner had to understand that this director would not be receptive to taking responsibility for any form of sales and marketing. Second, all the employees for this division had to be given a fair chance to remain with the new company. Third, I would offer my building and support services to keep the sold division going strong until the new buyer could take over totally. I simply did not want to sell the division and see it experience the typical gutting out or downsizing.

I found a buyer who shared my principles and the sale was completed. SACS supported the new company for three months after the sale by letting them use our offices, phones, support services, etc. It worked out so well that we decided to move into the same new building in the future when we changed our business location.

The second half of my tracking revealed that the current building we were utilizing was not being used to its full capacity. We discovered that we could operate the same operation out of 2,000 square feet, rather than 8,000 square feet. We found a new office complex in the same area that was willing to customize the inner office and training areas to our liking. I jumped at the chance.

I sold the current building at a price that paid off my existing loans and entered the new year of 1996 with a totally new, re-engineered business, a refreshed feeling, a new office complex, no serious cash flow/payroll problems, and a new team of key personnel who shared my excitement. I had learned the most important business lesson of my business career to date: *If you focus on the wrong set of numbers, it can become too late to recover from the snowballing effects of poor cash flow management*! Profit statements are not the only nor the first set of numbers to focus on. Cash flow problems are the #1 reason for the death of a business — not lack of profits!

A solid value of a closely held business lies in its ability to generate excess cash flow. If your business generates sales, has growth, but doesn't generate extra cash, the actual value of your business may be less than that of a company with flat sales and growth that generates a consistent flow of cash. Business experts place a strong value factor on businesses that have the ability to generate excess cash flow. *Remember: Small businesses have very few options for surviving a cash flow crisis!*

Instead of repeating myself in this chapter I am going to list several strong guidelines for avoiding cash flow problems as the lesson points to remember in the end as done in previous chapters:

Lesson #60: Reduce inventory levels.

Lesson #61: Avoid early payment discounts unless you are maintaining large sums of excess cash.

Lesson #62: Keep a continuous eye on accounts receivable and maintain strong credit and collections policy.

Lesson #63: Make sure you know the true costs of sales so that you can turn down unprofitable sales.

Lesson #64: Use payables to finance your investment in inventories (it's interest free).

Lesson #65: Your accounts payable status should equal your accounts receivables status.

Lesson #66: If you focus on the wrong set of numbers, it can become too late to recover from the snowballing effects of poor cash flow management.

Lesson #67: Remember: small businesses have very few options for surviving a cash flow crisis!

Rekindle The Fire

No matter how motivated you are, no matter how positive you are, no matter how driven you are, everyone needs to rekindle the fire from time to time! What exactly do I mean? It is tough to stay focused every single day on the job. Great leaders find a way to rekindle those fires and keep the desire burning. How can you accomplish such a goal?

There are several methods detailed in books on motivating employees. These books offer some great techniques that I have utilized. But I want to focus on one area that I feel does a great deal for keeping the fire burning: periodic training.

Several benefits grow from periodic training. First, the employee learns and the company gains. Second, the employees feel that you consider them important to the organization if you provide and pay for their training. Third, you rekindle the fire.

There is an extra advantage to continuous training. Not only do you acquire useful knowledge, but you meet other business associates. These business associates can be future customers and/or future contacts for your business needs. I have personally made some of my best contacts as a participant in a training program.

Many professional organizations provide a one or two hour training presentation. Many times it is just an interesting speaker who gives a "learning from experience" presentation. In my opinion, sending employees to these types of programs limits their time away from their job, assists in the learning process, exposes them to other potential clients/contacts, is very affordable and is a great marketing tool for your company.

The best solution is sending employees and yourself to different types of training as time and money permit. Don't make the mistake of thinking you can never afford the money or time. You can't afford *not* to spend the money or time on training, especially with the options available. I simply feel it is very important to get yourself and some of your employees out mixing, learning and indirectly marketing! It's a very effective way to *meet people, meet people, meet people*!

Lesson #68: No matter how motivated you are, no matter how positive you are, no matter how driven you are, everyone needs to rekindle the fire from time to time.

Lesson #69: The best solution is sending employees and yourself to different types of training as time and money permit.

Lesson #70: You can't afford *not* to spend the money or time on training, especially with the options available.

The Road To Motivation Simplified

1. **Most people want to do their job well.** This characteristic is very important and should be examined during the pre-employment review, with previous employers, and during the pre-employment testing and/or interview process. Once the employee is hired solid leadership will clearly define to all employees what the definition of "doing their job well" entails. Lastly, periodic review of each employee's job accomplishment is important.

2. **Most people want to succeed.** If each employee knows the definition of "doing their job well," we also have to make sure that the company provides employees with the chance for success. Provide the opportunity for employees to take pride in themselves, their jobs and their company. There is nothing worse than hindering an employee's success in accomplishing his/her job. This will end any chance of team spirit and, like poison, spread rapidly to other employees.

3. **Have open communications and listen to your employees.** You have to provide an open communications environment where new ideas can be heard and considered. If the suggestion cannot be implemented, a simple communication of why the idea can't be implemented can go a long way towards not discouraging future ideas from all employees.

4. **Most employees desire responsibility.** Assigning specific responsibilities to individual employees can result in a sense of self-importance and self-worth. True leaders never attempt to take all the responsibility, but share it. True leaders put their egos to the side and share the responsibility and successes!

5. **Employees need and desire achievement recognition.** Always take the opportunity to praise and award your employees. It is the simple rewards that mean the most such as a "thank you," public recognition, written "atta-boys," certificates of

praise, employee of the month awards, recognition at company meetings, monthly bonuses, etc.

Golden Rule: Employees need and want to be appreciated!

Know Thy Secretaries!

I learned early on that secretaries are the backbone of *all* businesses, not only my business. Many times they can be a significant part of the reason you initially get the opportunity to meet the decision makers and also are part of future decisions to utilize your business. If the secretary doesn't like you, it can have a significant impact on your future dealings with that company.

I have experienced, firsthand, business associates who treat secretaries with disrespect and I could predict the negative impact that would result for that associate.

The secretary controls several important aspects of the boss's business schedule. If you learn to work with the secretary you will gain a distinct advantage! Learn the secretary's first name and use it to your advantage. Write the secretary's name down on your contact's business card, in your card file and in your computer.

While cold calling in person I learned a very important lesson from a business associate who no longer is alive, but his methods are. He would leave each secretary a note pad of "things to do" lists. At the top and bottom of each page was a copy of his business card. Who does the boss ask to find and/or to call for many of his business needs? Guess what is conveniently sitting in front of the secretary every single day?

The bottom line is to leave the secretary with a positive and respectful feeling and you will get the same in return. The opposite is also true.

Lesson #71: Secretaries are the backbone of all businesses.

Lesson #72: If you learn to work with the secretary you will gain a positive advantage.

Lesson #73: Learn the secretary's name.

Lesson #74: Write the secretary's name down.

Lesson #75: Leave the secretary with a positive and respectful feeling and you will get the same in return.

The ABCs Of Successful Networking
At A Business Function

Many business professionals like the concept of networking, but find the experience unrewarding or uncomfortable. There are several guidelines that can make networking both productive and enjoyable.

The first and biggest mistake is that people view networking as an opportunity to get something for nothing. This reinforces what I stated in an earlier chapter — that this attitude gains you absolutely nothing. If this is your networking goal you will only be viewed as aggressive, abrasive and as having little interest in helping others.

To succeed in networking, both parties must benefit. It should be a win-win situation. It doesn't always equal out and at times you may give assistance without an immediate benefit returned. Other times, people help you and you can't return the favor. But, if you are persistent, it all balances out eventually for everyone.

You have to approach the networking opportunity with the proper attitude. If you are shy and never talk to anyone new at the networking function you are hindering your opportunities to expand your client and contact base.

If you are shy or have problems getting the engine running for networking, plan your networking experience just as seriously as you do any other business function.

Go to the function with an excited and positive attitude. That attitude will be displayed in your face, your voice, your gestures and (especially) your smile.

You need to work on your "thirty-second commercial" that explains to those you meet what your business does. Second, the thirty-second commercial has to be unique and "catchy" to make a strong impression.

When creating your thirty-second commercial make sure that you stress your business as a benefit. People use all business services because of the benefits derived from them. Make your line of work sound interesting instead of dull and boring.

Before you leave for the function count out five or ten business cards and tell yourself you can't leave the function until you meet enough other business professionals to hand out all your designated business cards.

Make your own permanent name tag that stands out and looks professional to wear for all of these events. Whether you use your own permanent name tag or one that is provided at the door, wear it on your right lapel. This makes it is easy to read when you shake someone's hand.

Walk around and make eye contact with as many people as you can. Remember, the majority of the business professionals present are there for the same reason: to meet potential new clients and business contacts. When you get a return of eye contact extend your hand and introduce yourself. First, show interest in the person you meet and their business. They will follow suit in most cases and ask what your line of work is; you can then proceed with your simple explanation. The beauty of this is that many times other people will be standing around, and they will be listening also. Attempt to include them in the conversation with eye contact, ask questions directed to them and provide them with your business cards. Don't forget to inquire about their business also. It is amazing how one action can lead to several business professionals interacting at a networking function.

Spend no more than 10-15 minutes with any one person at a networking function. If possible, go alone, or, if with someone else, split up until the event ends. Don't get into the habit of always needing to go to networking functions with business friends. Second, don't fall into the habit of always talking only to people you already know. Seek those you don't know and have never met.

Don't misunderstand what a successful "networking" experience is. If you walk out with a few or several NEW business contacts the key is that they are NEW. You can grow your business and at the same time assist others to expand their business. This is truly a "win-win" situation!

When you meet someone for the first time at a networking function take the time to read their business card. Second, make notes on the card so you'll remember who's who. Lastly, make sure you follow up with a phone call or short letter of appreciation that they took the time to meet and talk with you at the business function. You may want to include some additional information on your services along with the letter.

Networking at different events is very important since, as discussed before, business people desire to do business mainly with those they have met and liked! Lastly, don't forget that the "first impression" you make at a networking function is the *only* "first impression" you'll ever get with each new person you meet. Dress to make a strong and professional first impression.

Lesson #76: To succeed in networking both parties must benefit. It should be a win-win situation.

Lesson #77: Go to the function with an excited and positive attitude.

Lesson #78: Spend no more than 10-15 minutes with any one person at a networking function.

Lesson #79: Networking at different events is very important. Business people desire to do business mainly with those they have met and liked. Make a strong and professional first impression by the way you dress.

Your Company's First Impression

Many business owners and associates forget where their first impression is usually made — on the phone! How your business answers the phone is crucial. Many business owners give phone answering technique little consideration.

This means you have to train employees how to conduct themselves on the telephone. The phone needs to be answered promptly. Letting it ring too long gives the impression of not caring about the caller. The phone should also be answered with a cheerful attitude and a smile on your face. When teaching sales techniques on the phone I stress doing it with a smile. Can you tell if someone you talk to on the phone has a smile on their face? I can! In fact it is very obvious to me. The same rule applies to your office personnel answering the phone.

Additionally, the phone should be answered with a cheerful "good morning," or "good afternoon," your company name, and an offer such as "How can I help you?"

The person answering the phone should be prepared to respond to the caller's questions, and be able to route the call to the *right* person the *first* time! Last, only put a caller on hold when absolutely necessary — and then only after asking permission to do so.

Lesson #80: **Many business owners and associates forget where their first impression is usually made — on the phone.**

Lesson #81: **You have to train employees how to conduct themselves on the telephone.**

Lesson #82: The phone needs to be answered with a smile on your face and a cheerful attitude.

Lesson #83: Only put a caller on hold when absolutely necessary — and then only after asking permission to do so.

If You Want Your Company To Stand For Excellence...

1. **Know your product or service.** Knowledge or lack of it is a critical factor in the customer's appraisal of your performance.

2. **Know the customer's business.** The more your company and your employees know and understand about the customer's business, the more credible your company will be in the eyes of your customers.

3. **Give attention to detail.** Customers appreciate attention to detail. It will save your customers time and money, which creates value. Servicing the account as promised is imperative.

4. **Establish a TEAM attitude at your company.** TEAM stands for:

   T = **Together**
   E = **Everyone**
   A = **Achieves**
   M = **More**

5. **Keep your word.** The majority of surveys taken on successful leadership characteristics always discuss honesty and integrity. It is no different for businesses. Do you keep your word and deliver the service and/or product as initially promised? This comes down to one word that is very important in today's business world: reliability!

6. **Communicate with your customers.** Don't ever assume that your customers know what is going on. You should be communicating constantly with your customers. Let them know when things are not going exactly to plan, before you fail to achieve your promised service and/or product. And when things are going well check in with them and see if you can provide any additional needs. Once again I'll stress *"out of sight, out of mind."*

7. **Be responsive to your customers.** When customers have problems, they think of their most dependable service providers first. You have to be prepared and able to respond. You must always be accessible, available and willing to help customers whenever they have a problem.

8. **Be empathetic to your customers' needs.** You have to first listen to your customers and then make sure you are asking the right questions, speaking their language and tailoring your services to help them the best you can.

9. **Be universal with your customer.** Your customer's opinion and level of confidence in your services/products can be affected by everything they see, feel, touch, hear and smell concerning your business. Each experience will make an impression, either for better or worse.

10. **Be credible and reliable.** Customers are willing to pay for peace of mind. Customers are always willing to return to people and businesses that want to help and have their customers' best interest at heart.

* **Taking reliable care of your customers is what keeps them buying, multiplying, referring and coming back.**

Using Your Customers' Eyes

An extensive newspaper article was written about my company, my background and how SACS Consulting got started and grew over the years. I obviously utilize this article for marketing purposes. But, one day I decided to frame a copy of it and hang it in my reception area. I really didn't think it would attract much attention but thought it gave our company some extra credibility if anyone cared to read it.

I also have a security camera system set up in my building so that I can view the reception area any time I need to. I would observe clients, friends and business associates entering the reception area and, without fail, almost all the visitors would read that article. When I greeted them, the very first thing they would comment on was the article and the information contained in it. Basically, the article provided some preliminary information on the company, our growth, etc. that the visitors in most cases didn't know. Last, everyone who read the article was very impressed; without a doubt, the article raised our level of professionalism in the reader's mind. It was such a small thing, but it made such a large impact!

I have to admit that I now allow all visitors a few minutes to read the article. The article also saves me time in explaining all the details about my company, how it started, and how we have grown. The article spotlights the company as a "success story in the making." You can't spend enough money to achieve that reputation!

I also noticed different companies with articles on their reception area walls. I have also visited companies that leave a three-ring binder out with examples of their work, pictures of the inner workings of their business and copies of testimonials from satisfied customers. When I enter a business I instantly look for these items because I want to learn more about the company I'm visiting.

Use the eyes of your clients in the reception area. It is one more tool at your disposal that should not be ignored nor the opportunity wasted.

Lesson #84: Use your customer's eyes to benefit your company.

Lesson #85: Utilize the eyes of your clients in the reception area.

Why Customers Quit

A successful business owner knows the value of keeping current customers satisfied and the potential they possess for future repeat sales and/or service. Did you know the typical business receives a minimum of 60% of their future repeat business from current clients? Make sure you understand this concept when addressing your future business plans and when a decision has to be made on prioritizing. Who should be given the highest priority? Finally, who do you think provides most of the leads (referrals) for the remaining 40% of your future business?

A study by the White House Office of Consumer Affairs has researched and developed some very interesting and informative information concerning "Why Customers Quit."

Why Customers Quit:

3%   Move away
5%   Develop other friendships (other business)
9%   Leave for competitive reasons
14% Are dissatisfied with the product
68% Quit because of an attitude of indifference toward them by the owner, manager or some other employees

Typically:

1. Dissatisfied customers will tell eight to ten people about the problem.

2. One in five dissatisfied customers will tell twenty other people.

3. It takes twelve positive service incidents to make up for one negative incident.

4. Seven out of ten complaining customers will do business with you again if you resolve the complaint in their favor.

5. If you resolve the complaint on the spot, 95% will do business with you again.

6. On average, a satisfied complainer will tell five people about the problem and how it was satisfactorily resolved.

7. Dissatisfied customers seldom complain, don't come back, and don't hesitate to spread the news in an exaggerated fashion.

Typically:

1. A business will hear from only 4% of its dissatisfied customers.

2. The other 96% of dissatisfied customers just quietly go away.

3. 91% of unhappy customers will never come back.

The Average Business:

1. Spends 6 times more to attract new customers than it does to keep old ones.

2. Finds that a customer's loyalty is, in most cases, worth 10 times the price of a single purchase.

Lesson #86: Remember: if you don't provide quality customer service, someone else will.

Lesson #87: Every company's greatest asset is its satisfied customers.

Lesson #88: You will obtain 60% of future sales from present customers.

Lesson #89: Focus on what customers want and need.

Lesson #90: Make helping the customer the top priority in your job.

Lesson #91: The greatest customer must first be yourself.

Lesson #92: Remember that emotions are contagious.

Lesson #93: Customers remember 80% of what they see versus 20% of what they hear.

Lesson #94: When working with your customers, use problems as opportunities to demonstrate just what great service your company can provide.

"The Leader" vs. "The Boss"

1. **Be a leader, not just a boss.** Bosses tell workers what to do, rely heavily on inspection and utilize force to make employees do what they are told. Leaders are open and have ongoing discussions with employees on most aspects of the business, including reducing costs, improving quality, etc. Leaders listen and allow employees to talk and listen. Leaders support management and employees becoming one team with common goals.

2. **Leaders show by example and empower others.** Leaders show employees how, rather than just *telling* them how to do the job. Leaders support ongoing training. Leaders encourage others to be creative and empower others to take active roles within the company. Leaders don't procrastinate and don't allow others to procrastinate either. Leaders know that you must understand yourself in order to better understand and empower others. Leaders understand that part of empowerment can involve delegating responsibilities to the right people and then supporting them actively.

3. **Leaders support and encourage self-inspection.** Encourage your employees to do their own inspections. Employees become more responsible for the quality of their work, and they are more accountable. Leaders understand, expect and are prepared to deal with problems. Bosses hope that problems never surface and when problems exist they are totally unprepared. A strong leader can show his employees that being unprepared for problems is the worst problem that can exist.

4. **The entire company values constant improvement.** If the leader values improvement and instills that value in employ-

ees, it will grow. The company must provide both the tools and support for improvements. The entire team focuses on the goals of the company with a "we" attitude rather than an "I" or "me" attitude.

5. **Leaders have a vision.** Leaders have a definitive vision of how everything fits together. The vision is a dream with a detailed plan. The vision has a clear understanding of the path to success. A leader considers every decision from every angle. Leaders don't give up and don't give in. The leader possesses a high level of commitment to the concept of the company. A leader sees "The Big Picture" of the company and industry and wants it more than anything!

6. **Leaders are focused for the long run.** Leaders have a clear, long range focus for their individual and company goals. Bosses have short, narrow focuses — or no focus at all. The boss only focuses on personal goals without regard for the company as a whole or the individual employees. Leaders understand and believe that each individual is in total control of his/her own destiny. You cannot knock leaders off track while they are focused on their long range goals. Obstacles are only temporary delays and learning experiences to leaders. To bosses, obstacles are reasons to quit and blame the failures on others or on circumstances beyond their control. A leader always stays focused and help others stay focused. A boss will not stay focused and rarely helps others stay focused. Leaders are relentless in their ability to stay focused on their vision and always begin with an end in mind. Leaders always keep on trying, no matter how hard it seems.

7. **Leaders are always pro-active.** Leaders are always pro-active instead of reactive. Leaders want to be the first to attempt new products and services. They are the first to allow new ideas from employees to be reviewed. Leaders are always attempting to prevent problems from surfacing in the future. Leaders learn from setbacks so that it doesn't happen again and they

improve from the experience. Leaders will seek first to understand and then will make decisions. Leaders know they must take some chances, but only after considerable debate, review and experimentation. Leaders realize that if the majority of the time they are only in a reactive mode, time will slowly destroy all the positive in their organization. Leaders realize that being pro-active means they must adopt a win/win attitude.

8. **Leaders know and accept their personal limitations**. A strong leader does not have to be able to "do it all." A leader knows and accepts his/her personal limitations and seeks those who can complement those weaknesses. A leader trusts his/her intuitive directions and acts on them with confidence and consistency. A leader believes in himself 100%. A strong leader does not have an ego that needs to be stroked!

9. **Leaders surround themselves with successful people.** If you want to be successful, surround yourself with other successful people. Success is just as contagious as negativity. History has shown repeatedly that successful people of the past mimicked and learned from other successful people. Leaders develop successful habits from observing other successful people. Leaders ignore those who try to discourage them. As the saying goes, "Why reinvent the wheel?" Leaders avoid negative sources, people, places, things and habits.

10. **Leaders know how to deal with change.** Leaders realize that change can be very hard for employees and customers to accept. Leaders realize that the best method for preparing people for change is to advise everyone that the change is coming long before it happens. Leaders then make the change and follow up by informing how the change is working. Lastly, leaders seek input before, during and after the change takes place. Leaders realize that people hate negative surprises!

11. **Leaders have unique human characteristics.** Leaders separate themselves from the rest with a few certain unique charac-

teristics. They work both hard and smart. They always strive to be on time as arranged. They always attempt to return every phone call. They keep their word and they honor people. They take on the hardest job first. They can do two or three things at once very well. They lead with kindness and are very enthusiastic. They *say* negatives and *write* positives. Most of all, revenge is never on their minds. They always attempt to find something positive in everyone and desire to build bridges, trying never to destroy bridges.

12. **Leader realize that at times you must stand alone.** In my opinion, this is the toughest part of being a true leader. There will always be times in a leader's life when he/she will have to make a decision and carry through by themselves. There may be times when a leader will be alone in a decision because he or she is the only one who truly has full understanding of the situation. A leader has to be strong enough (and willing) to stand alone before he or she can truly be regarded as one of the better leaders of our time.

* **Leaders must be multi-faceted in their abilities. A pencil without an eraser can only perform one function.**

* **In my opinion the greatest challenge in life is creating a friendship with an adversary. Only leaders would think of achieving this and only leaders could make it happen.**

Can A Company Grow Too Quickly?

This is a situation that many business owners believe could never happen. They believe that fast growth equates with bigger profits. This is not necessarily true since, as discussed previously in this book, cash flow, personnel abilities, etc. can be real concerns for a company that grows too fast.

I experienced fast growth in my company. When I finally realized what was taking place, I had to stop and realign several aspects of my business. I also had to cease taking on additional business until we got caught up. Who would ever dream that in less than five years I would be dealing with this type of business problem?

The basic signs that indicate a company is growing too quickly are:

1. Employees are working in positions beyond their abilities.

2. Employee turnover increases.

3. Too many people report to the owner.

4. Customers begin complaining about late and/or incomplete orders or service.

5. Old processes can't keep up with new demands.

6. The company can't pay bills on time, even though sales increase.

7. Cash flow slows.

8. The company seems to be in constant crisis.

9. The owner spends too much time fighting fires.

10. The owner doesn't enjoy running the business anymore.

One Of The Hardest Decisions
Owners Need To Make:
Can You Make It?

My original secretary was a hard worker and worked out fine until I added several employees who required interaction and co-operation. My first director was doing a fine job until we added the responsibility of supervising numerous employees. Another director did a good job until the ability to abuse time became a regular habit. All three of these key employees are now gone, but I should have corrected the situation much earlier. My lack of experience and knowledge in this area hindered me tremendously.

On the other hand, I had a director who was a good employee, but lacked the needed sales and marketing ability that my company needed (which he admitted he did not possess). I sold that division with the strong recommendation that he be the key district manager for that company, to accent his strengths.

Finally, I had a few key employees who moved on to other jobs, pursuing the opportunities to potentially better themselves. I always supported their decisions and gave them the encouragement to work hard for their personal goals. I had a key employee who started out as my secretary and eventually worked so hard she moved up to become a very important and key employee as my office manager and payroll specialist. She desired a change and I had no choice but to support her decision. Sometimes the company can't satisfy an employee's financial and/or personal challenge needs, so changes should take place.

When my company first began, I was obviously involved in all the decisions. I had contact with all clients for two years, until the company grew to the point where I needed to delegate some of those responsibilities to other key employees. Delegating authority was one of the first difficult tasks for me to learn. This is very true for many other new business owners. To succeed and support strong growth, delegating is a must.

The next difficult decision is to be able to recognize that with growth also comes the need for key employees to be responsible for accepting added responsibilities and meeting rising expectations. But, most of all, these key employees must have the ability and knowledge to carry the expanded responsibilities. In many cases the employee won't have the knowledge and/or ability to expand along with the company. This does not mean that the key employee is not a hard worker, it simply means that he or she just doesn't have what it takes. This person simply becomes overwhelmed and underperforming.

I have talked to numerous owners who have stated that this decision is one of the toughest to make. They have also made me aware that this situation takes place more often than I ever realized. Most of the time owners attempt to work around this situation, hoping that it will work itself out. Or the owner attempts to provide training to the key employee with the hope that this will fix the situation. Only in a few situations does the training solve the situation. CEOs and other managers must be able to recognize when a key employee can't keep up.

The reason this situation is so tough to resolve is because that employee, in many cases, has been with you from the early inception of the company or at least for several years. Additionally, friendships may have been developed with the key employee and their family members.

Why does this problem occur so frequently? At the inception of the new company entrepreneurs focus getting their business off the ground. Naturally, they often hire people based on current needs and focus more on personality rather than ability. As the company grows the key employee is unprepared to handle the increasing responsibility being assigned to them.

In reality you are doing the employee a major disservice by keeping them in that position. Ignoring the situation can fuel more problems, such as morale issues, tensions, productivity problems, internal relationship problems, etc. The bottom line is that if you let it keep going on, it only gets worse! It is much better to deal with it promptly, honestly and directly. Don't keep underperformers in their current positions.

Owners/managers need to get the key employee out of that job position for the sake of the company *and* for the employee's emotional survival. It is more humane to reassign the key employee within the company or let them go with some form of outplacement service than to let the situation fester. Just because the key employee didn't work out for your company does not mean that they cannot work out in another company. Otherwise, as time goes on, the situation will turn into poison, and will spread among other employees, clients and the overall service provided.

There are also situations where employees cannot move up within the company. Owners and CEOs must realize these employees should not be promoted beyond their level of competence. Simply stated, there is nothing wrong with this realization.

Several CEOs have informed me that such employees have even thanked them for forcing the decision and helping them move on with their lives. Many times these key employees knew in their heart and soul they weren't getting the job done and they needed a change!

Lesson #95: **To succeed and support strong growth, delegating is a must.**

Lesson #96: **With growth also comes the need for key employees to be responsible for accepting added responsibilities and meeting rising expectations.**

Lesson #97: **CEOs and other managers must be able to see when a key employee can't keep up.**

Lesson #98: **Don't keep underperformers in their current positions.**

Lesson #99: Just because the employee didn't work out for your company does not mean that they cannot work out in another company.

Lesson #100: Employees should not be promoted beyond their level of competence.

Lesson #101: Many times key employees know in their heart and soul they aren't getting the job done and they need a change.

What Does Being A Business Owner Really Mean?

I met an interesting business professional who became a very good friend and business contact. Her name is Patti Noussias, owner of Creative Training Concepts, located in Akron, Ohio. She specializes in training programs for businesses. Additionally, she is working on a very informative book dealing with business start-up. One section of the book deals with what being an owner really means. Patti stresses that, primarily, businesses fail because of a lack of knowledge, planning, capital, management skills and vision. With her permission I am reprinting her list of:

How Business Owners Differ From Others

* As a business owner, you're accountable for making decisions — whether they're right or wrong.

* As a business owner, you're responsible for becoming disciplined to work independently and without a boss.

* As a business owner, you're liable for all legal and financial matters.

* As a business owner, you will learn that even though you are fabulous in your area of expertise, if you don't learn fast enough or find someone with the knowledge you need in ALL of the other areas of business management, your business could suffer undue damage.

* As a business owner, you're probably not going to see a steady flow of money into your business; rather, you're going to see an up and down roller coaster of sales and income.

*   As a business owner, the 8 to 5 routine will completely change to include early morning and late evening hours, too.

*   As a business owner, you might realize that stable sales don't happen often in the first few years of business. *EGADS!*

*   As a business owner, you will discover that others do not view your wonderful product/service with as much wonder as you do.

*   As a business owner, you will learn that there truly are people who will help you if you will just ask them.

*   As a business owner, you will find people who say they will help you and then actually end up hurting your business and costing you a great deal of money.

*   As a business owner, you will rejoice over all of the great moments of success and the triumph of making a big sale.

*   As a business owner, you will also have to learn how to overcome the agony of a lost sale, the bitterness of rejection, and the sorrow of a slow month.

*   As a business owner, you will face ALL of your fears head on.

*   As a business owner, there may be several times when you will want to quit.

*   And as many business owners, faced with financial struggles, legal hassles, and low sales have said, you will say to yourself in the mirror...

    "Yes, but this FREEDOM is worth it. I'll stay in business one more month..."

If You Want A Piece Of The Pie, You Must First Create The Pie

As a business owner everyone makes mistakes, including myself. I discussed employee motivation and dedication with other business owners until I was blue in the face. Being a consultant has provided me with the opportunity to travel throughout the U.S. and experience companies internally, firsthand, as I worked with and trained both supervisors and employees. The most satisfied employees and supervisors, the most profitable businesses had one dominant aspect in common.

Second, through the years I have talked with my employees and numerous employees of other businesses. These discussions have revealed differences of opinion, theory, motivation, dedication, effective business practices, etc. Once again, the same dominant aspect stood out with the more successful companies.

Third, I have researched and read several books on the subject of employee motivation and dedication. My research and review of these books has revealed some interesting basic facts, but one factor stood out again as crucial.

What was this one dominant factor? It was the simple fact that the more successful, positive and satisfied employees were found at companies structured so that *everyone had something at stake*! This tied in with the TEAM-oriented business where groups of employees worked their schedules out, were accountable to each other and had to rely on each other. This also tied in with the companies whose employees earned monthly, quarterly or yearly bonuses based on the profit-loss statements. This also tied in with companies whose management, sales, marketing, production, shipping, etc. all received a base pay along with an additional portion of their pay tied to *results*! In certain job categories (sales, marketing, directors, etc.) base pay would be smaller with a larger portion of their pay tied to the incentive-results part of their pay. In other types of job categories (production, shipping, etc.) base pay would be larger with a smaller portion of pay tied into the incentive-results part of their pay. Either way everyone has something at stake and everyone has continuous incentive to work hard!

The bottom line: the most satisfied employee companies (which ironically were the most financially successful companies I experienced and worked with) had all the employees working with one thought in mind: If I create the pie first, then I can have a piece of it!

The piece you get could be as large as you want it to be. I found out that the employees in these businesses did simple things such as turning lights off in rooms when they were not in use. They were much more careful about waste and finding more use for byproducts. The degree of customer satisfaction grew tremendously. These employees do all the little things because they want to, not because they are told to. Theses employees have more pride than other employees working next door to them. The creative juices flow and self-monitoring expands to new heights. The company experiences positive action and attitude throughout all aspects of its operations and service!

Today's employee is definitely of a different breed with different motivation needs. Simply put, today's employees work their best and hardest when they have a piece of ownership — the ability to own a piece of the pie — and are given the responsibility and opportunity to determine their financial success within the company.

The last piece of this puzzle is that your recruitment of employees needs to include only those applicants who are excited about being part of this working environment. The positive aspect of this type of working environment is that if a certain employee doesn't buy into this type of program you won't have to terminate that employee, because his or her co-workers won't allow the problem to continue on their nickel!

Lesson #102: The more successful, positive and satisfied employee companies are structured so that everyone has something at stake.

Lesson #103: Today's employees work their best and hardest when they have a piece of ownership — the ability to own a piece of the pie — and are given the responsibility and opportunity to determine their financial success within the company.

Lesson #104: Your recruitment of employees needs to include only those applicants who are excited about being part of this working environment.

The following pages were contributed by David B. Nicholson. His insight and experience can be very valuable to the success and growth of your business!

Profit Is Not A Dirty Word

While you as a new business person may think your intelligence is being insulted by the title of this chapter, ask any failed business owner (or one who was at the brink of failure) and they will tell you that not understanding profits was the reason for their troubles.

Many individuals going into business do not initially understand the types of profits needed to sustain a business, nor do they know how to formulate a plan for adequate profits to ensure the continued success of the business. Let's discuss gross profit and net profit.

Gross Profits

Gross profits are the monies left over from deducting the initial costs of doing business, i.e., the cost of the product or service. Gross profit is usually calculated on a 65% - 35% "spread" or "margin" basis. This means 65% of your per unit price or total sales go towards the cost of the item and/or wages. The 35% left over goes toward paying any expenses for overhead, taxes, supplies, etc.

The pitfall many business owners run into is that they may fail to generate adequate gross profits. Why? Because they did not fully understand their business needs to begin with at start up. Depending on your type of business, gross profit needs can vary widely.

The biggest and most often misunderstood factor in new start-up businesses is that overhead costs were not calculated properly or that the costs were allowed to get out of control. The business owner may not have monitored operations properly or planned for contingencies that ultimately came to influence the business. For the small business owner this spells death to the business. So, how do you avoid inadequate gross profits?

First, develop a business plan. If you do not know how, get someone who has a track record of business success to show you how. Talk to others in similar businesses. Gather competitive intelligence on those who will ultimately be your competition. Research trends within the marketplace as those trends may have an effect on your business. Are you coming into an emerging market or one that has been served for a period of time? What new technological developments are out there? How will those developments affect your business when they become available? Unless you are blessed enough to be the inventor or sole patent holder of the most unique product or service in the world, do not underestimate your competition!

Second, develop a budget or model of your business based on projected sales (revenues) for the first, second and third years. If you have done adequate market research you should be able to forecast with some degree of accuracy how your business should progress. Why? Look at the large, multi-dimensional corporations and franchises. Market research is one of the key elements in their quest for market share and sustained growth. While you may never achieve the heights of success that the "big boys" do, why shouldn't you use some of the same tools they use to achieve your own level of success?

Third, once you have opened the doors understand that you as the business owner will now wear many hats. You are the president, bookkeeper, sales and marketing rep, stock boy, customer service rep, etc. Depending on your business, you may be the only one generating income or overseeing others who generate income for you. The one thing you cannot lose sight of is generation of gross profit. Absentee business owners are rarely successful (or only achieve such status after years of hard work and very strict accountability controls).

Gross profits ultimately produce net profits, but only if the gross profits were adequate. Controlling costs ensures that there will be a net profit and that you have formulated a realistic business plan. This gets back to being knowledgeable from the outset about ALL aspects of your business, being informed and aware of ALL factors that could adversely affect your business and sticking to your business plan ALL of the time.

While it may be necessary to hire help to run your business remember that your employees do not have a vested interest in your business. The employee very rarely understands the intricacies of business. The average employee never sees the bills, tax assessments and rent due every month. Consequently, the employee does not care if the light burns when no one is around, that the thermostat is left on 78 degrees at night when no one is there, or that carelessness in handling your inventory resulted in damaged product that could not be sold. Hey, look at all that money you put in the bank. Hey, you can deduct it from your taxes. The fact is, that waste is net profit and could be the determining factor between success and failure. Your only insurance is accountability and sticking to that game plan. That means long hours devoted to the business.

Things you need to take into consideration for your business plan are wages, rent or bank notes, taxes, cost of supplies and merchandise, if applicable. Numerous factors can result in adverse sales. Are you prepared for drastic changes in business conditions? Increased competition because you opened your business in a market previously dominated by one company? A major road closed for repaving which results in an inconvenience to your customers? Weather, natural disasters, and civil disorders can all influence your business. How would you deal with them?

Knowing where your money is going is the single most important aspect of running your business! Are you paying too much in wages? Rent? For raw material? By having a budget and working with an accountant you can keep control of your costs and profits. No one today can afford to "fly" their business by the seat of their pants. *Finding ways to do business at less cost while maintaining service and quality to your customers is the greatest challenge the business owner has today.* You would not set out on a trip to unknown territory without a map and a plan. Your business plan and market research are your guides to success. Success is only realized when NET PROFITS are generated.

How you capitalize your business will be a factor in your success. But knowing your business and controlling that capital and its use wisely will ensure that travelling the road to success is a smooth one.

There are many variations on how a detailed business plan should be developed and how strictly it should be followed. Again, seeking counsel from someone knowledgeable is your best bet to getting back on track if you have derailed, or staying on track if you think you are getting ready to jump the tracks. *Either way, adaptability to changing conditions and continuing analysis of your business should be, and is, the key to success.*

A good business plan will develop a model of your projected sales into certain percentages against your expenses. For example, using the 65-35 factor, the 35% gross profit may have 6% allocated to overhead wages, such as for a secretary and receptionist. Knowing that the telephone will be used, especially long distance services, 8% of your sales may be allocated to this service. The "trick" is that you have a net profit left over after paying the bills in your model. Assuming you have not miscalculated greatly in your model, the actual percentage figures developed by your accountant every month will give you an idea of what areas of expenses, if any, are out of line with the model. The model also "tells" you what you are going to charge customers for your goods or services. Will those prices be in line with your competition? If more, what justifies your increased costs? Will the public pay those costs based on the justification?

The business plan includes your research into the competition. Is it thorough? Is it realistic? Has your desire to "cash in" on what you have perceived as the "chance of a lifetime" clouded your vision as to the reality of the business climate? What about market saturation? Remember, you not only have competitors, you are *their* competition also! What unknown factors exist? While it is impossible to know they are coming, how are you going to react to unexpected situations? You cannot just ignore them; the bank, you will find, is not going to be very sympathetic when you start missing payments. Nor will your other creditors. KNOW YOUR BUSINESS! Ask yourself "Will I be able to survive on these profits?"

While you do not have to be a pessimist to be in business you must be able to SUCCESSFULLY adapt to changing conditions and circumstances.

Be innovative! Be flexible! Just because it has been done that way for a hundred years does not mean you have to continue doing so — but make sure you can do it *at a profit*.

Unless you are starting a business venture that the world has never seen before, certain principles apply to all businesses. For the small business owner it is a relatively straightforward process.

Your business plan defines your course of growth for the short and long term objectives you may have in mind. The percentage figures you develop as part of the financial aspect of your business become indicators that you may be wandering into dangerous territory or exceeding profit objectives. Understand that percentage allocations to all aspects of your business allow for swift analysis of your monthly figures. If your percentages aren't within those budgeted then you had better find out where the money went and take steps to stop or recover the loss.

Experienced business owners can tell you on a daily or weekly basis whether they are within their budget. Some do so by daily bookkeeping records based on past sales data. If you have overspent in an area in a given month, was that expense a one time charge or was it an ongoing charge? Extraordinary expenses that are not ongoing may benefit your business in the long run, so do not panic when such items appear on your profit-and-loss statement. Just be sure you know where that money went and why it was spent. The purpose of your budget is to make sure you are not continually overspending for items you may not need.

Inventory control is very important. Most businesses only do one inventory a year. Depending on your business, inventory should be done at least twice a year, if not more often. This summary should be reconciled with your profit-and-loss statements to ensure you do not have employees pilfering your stock or shoplifters stealing you blind.

Many business owners end up in trouble because they allow profits to be devoured by unsound business practices. In starting out, the business owner usually knows that he will face some rough times while trying to establish a customer base. But as time goes on, the business owner may not be aware of (or ignores) trends, although he develops some loyalty to his employees A slump in business revenues may be viewed as a temporary condition and the owner does not lay off the employees or cut back on such expenses by reducing hours — the employees' or the business'. When it becomes apparent that recovery is not going to occur, it may be too late to salvage the business. Profits were used to keep things going when it may have been a better decision to have eliminated employees, either by layoffs or attrition. Reducing hours that the business was open may have saved additional utility expenses as well as reducing payroll and associated expenses.

An aspect of business that may be eating away at profits is that the business owner is spending time doing work that takes away from his primary purpose — making money for the business. Can someone else do what the owner is doing? Can it be contracted out to a service company? Conversely, are you contracting out to a service for things that you can do yourself? Is the value received tangible — in the form of profits generated from your having been relieved of this aspect of the business? Remember, money spent in your pursuit of business was derived from one of two sources, working capital or profits. Every dollar spent should have first been viewed from the aspect of that dollar contributing to making additional dollars. If spending the money is not going to make you money then DON'T SPEND IT!

Business is business. Friendships and support of worthy causes are fine if you are making money over and above your plan. There will always be a time when you will have to draw a line because a friend or someone else will try to play upon your sense of decency or goodwill. Don't fall into that trap! Be firm. Your survival is at stake.

Up to this point, assuming that you have read this far, you are saying to yourself "This is awfully redundant." No one is going to argue the point. However, any successful business owner will tell you that the points made over and over again cannot be stressed enough. Anyone who has failed in business will usually admit that they can trace their failure to not being knowledgeable enough about

116

their business. Yes, they may blame other influences in public but when alone, and not fearing being quoted in public, most will admit that they neglected some aspect, or many aspects, of their business. There are failures from circumstances beyond control, such as natural disaster. These are few and far between.

Profits are generated from knowing your business and your competition — and from working long, hard hours at keeping control of your business. Planning and execution of the plan bring success. But what happens when you think you are doing all the right things and the profits are not there?

Get out your profit-and loss statements. Analyze them. Are your costs in line with your model or budget? Are your overhead expenses more than you projected? Are you spending too much in wages? Utilities? Are your sales justified in relation to these expenses and vice versa? Being familiar with your business plan will help you identify which areas need corrective action. Your accountant should also be feeding back information indicating courses of action to be pursued. Remember, there are only three things that can be done to correct losses:

1. Reduce overhead expenses.
2. Raise prices for goods and/or services.
3. Reduce wages and associated expenses.

Now, of the three, none is preferable. In most cases, a smart business owner will try a combination of the three, so that the end result is not so drastic as to disrupt the business to the point of failure.

You, the business owner, must also have realistic expectations of the profits that can be generated from your business. That gets back to knowing your business and knowing about the business (your competition) in general.

The well-developed business plan is based on knowledge (see above). This knowledge translates into profit, gross and net. So, now you ask, "What kind (or how much) gross and net profits do I need?" Only you, *after* you have a business plan (*knowledge*), can determine those needs.

It was previously mentioned that a rule of thumb was 65% - 35%. Your business needs may dictate that "spreads" or "margins" be more. A need for premium business quarters could be a factor. Thus your need for more gross profits to offset the costs. The need to pay higher wages could increase your needs. It all gets back to *knowledge* and knowing your needs. This can only be accomplished by research and then developing a realistic business plan.

Remember, PROFIT is not a dirty word — it is your key to remaining in business!

SACS Speaker/Training Topics

Tim Dimoff travels extensively to provide information and entertaining training sessions and/or presentations to professional groups throughout the U.S. All training sessions and/or presentations can be tailored to your group and adjusted according to your time requirements. Here is a sampling of topics:

Workplace Issues and Employee Confrontations — This program focuses on dealing with the employee who is exhibiting poor job performance and/or is failing to adhere to safety procedures. This program emphasizes procedures concerning proper observation, confronting, documentation, follow-up and liability reduction techniques for management and supervision.

Drugs and Alcohol in the Workplace — A discussion of the many legal considerations must be addressed when developing a drug and alcohol policy. This discussion includes indicators that point to drug and alcohol use in the workplace, how to implement an effective training program, ways to reduce company liability, court decisions and case laws.

Violence in the Workplace — How to prevent, diffuse and recover from workplace violence incidents. This presentation includes how to identify tendencies towards violent behavior, your liability as an employer, preventive security and effective employee screening.

Sexual Harassment in the Workplace — A review of current state and federal laws pertaining to sexual harassment in the workplace, along with supervisory training methods and policy development that will prevent sexual harassment. Proper reporting, investigating and disciplining of sexual harassment incidents will also be covered.

Avoiding Common Pitfalls with Applicants and Current Employees — This is a comprehensive review of the Americans with Disabilities Act, and other state and federal requirements' impact on the hiring process. It offers alternative methods for pre-employment reviews including background checks, testing and interviewing. Additionally, this program reviews proper methods for observing, confronting, documenting and controlling current employee workplace issues and confrontations.

How to Motivate Your Employees — A variety of interesting, inexpensive and proven methods used by corporations across the U.S. to motivate employees.

The Impact of Americans with Disabilities Act (ADA) — An explanation of the new ADA guidelines and solutions for applying them to your hiring process, employee advancement, facility, etc. Also included are suggested changes to your employment application and management programs to reduce the potential of litigation.

Networking: The Ultimate Warrior — Tim Dimoff presents his winning formula for making and increasing the contacts that can be the key to your company's growth. Hear how this networking system enabled his company to grow from one to 150 employees, and five divisions with offices in three major cities, in less than five years.

Addiction and its Impact — This explanation of the addictive powers and allure of crack cocaine, powder cocaine and methamphetamine (ice) includes showing samples of these drugs and discussing the monetary incentives of selling them.

Crime Prevention for your Home, Auto and Family — This program teaches common sense techniques to reduce your chances of being the next victim. Effective physical security methods, high-tech security equipment and a variety of door locking systems will be explained and on hand for viewing.

Department of Transportation Update — This seminar is geared toward companies with 50 or fewer employees and focuses on DOT alcohol and drug testing, pre-employment testing, and guidelines. The seminar also touches on company policy requirements, training requirements, and documentation.

The YOU In Business — Tim's national seller on how to build a strong business from the inside out and take the lead in your area of expertise. Tim has developed this topic into a national selling book and cassette.

Dock and Warehouse Theft — Learn about the reasons for dock and warehouse theft and effective preventive procedures to eliminate these types of thefts.

Smart Hiring — Learn the Do's and Don'ts of employee recruitment and selection with emphasis on the guidelines for selecting the right employee for the job.

Self-defense and Assault Prevention for Women — A discussion that will prepare women to protect themselves against crime and to make their homes, offices and vehicles safer.

Personal Safety for Women Who Travel — Learn how women can protect themselves for safer traveling.

For additional copies of this book, to purchase book on cassette, or to arrange for Tim Dimoff to present a speech or seminar, contact:

Timothy A. Dimoff
c/o SACS Consulting
400 N. Cleveland Ave.
Mogadore, OH 44260

Phone: 330-628-6393
FAX: 330-628-6641
Toll Free: 1-888-722-7937
E-Mail: TADimoff@sacsconsulting.com
Web Page: www.sacsconsulting.com

Order Info:

BERGDORF COMPANY
3803 State Road, Akron, OH 44319-2131
Phone: 330-644-4444 FAX: 330-644-4363
1-800-968-3735

Speaker Info:

www.sacsconsulting.com
TADimoff@sacsconsulting.com
1-888-722-7937
Phone: 330-628-6393 FAX: 330-628-6641

ORDER FORM

Date Ordered: _____

Name: _____

Address: _____
All orders will be shipped via UPS. No P.O. boxes, please

City: _____ State: _____ Zip: _____

Phone: _____
In case we have a question about your order.

NO OF ITEMS	DESCRIPTION	CHECK ONE			PRICE	TOTAL
		BOOK	VIDEO	CASSETTE		
	How To Recognize Substance Abuse	X			14 95	
	The YOU In Business	X			14 95	
	The YOU In Business			X	14 95	
	Life Rage	X			14.95	

Shipping & Handling Charges:	
1 item: $ 3 00	SUBTOTAL
2-5 items: $ 4 75	OH Residents add 5 75% sales tax
6-10 items: $ 7 25	
11-25 items $10 75	Shipping/Handling
Over 26 items, call for price discount	TOTAL

Check Enclosed _____ M/C _____ Visa _____ Amex _____

Signature: _____ Exp. Date _____

Comments: _____